LET'S GO DEEPER

J. LEE GRADY

CHARISMA
HOUSE

Back cover photo by Vadim Paripa

Visit the author's website at https://leegrady.com.

Cataloging-in-Publication Data is on file with the Library of Congress.
International Standard Book Number: 978-1-63641-126-2
E-book ISBN: 978-1-63641-127-9

22 23 24 25 26 — 9876543
Printed in the United States of America

Contents

How to Use This Study

WHETHER YOU RECENTLY decided to follow Jesus Christ or have been a Christian for a while and you want to reacquaint yourself with the basic truths of your faith, I'm excited you are making the journey to study this book.

Let's Go Deeper is designed to equip and inspire you in your relationship with God. It's divided into thirty short lessons covering all the fundamental beliefs of Christianity. You can read this book alone if you prefer, but it will be more meaningful if you study it with a small group of other believers.

My goal is that this book will build a strong spiritual foundation in your life and help you grow in your relationship with Jesus. The Bible compares new Christians to infants, who need nourishment and care. The apostle Peter told his disciples: "Like newborn babies, long for the pure milk of the word, so that by it you may grow in respect to salvation" (1 Peter 2:2).

If you want to grow as a disciple of Jesus you must have spiritual hunger. You must "long for the pure milk of the word." If you approach this study with intense passion, God will satisfy your desire and reveal His truth to you. Read each lesson carefully, study the Bible verses, and respond to the questions at the end of each lesson. Also, if you are doing this study with a small group, you can use the "Let's Talk About It" question at the end of each lesson as a springboard for conversation.

Make sure you also read the short biographies of Bible characters at the beginning of each lesson. These are called "Heroes of Our Faith." The Bible is full of stories of ordinary people who were transformed because they met the Lord and followed Him. They lived long ago, but their lives are still examples to us. Their experiences will inspire you and give you some helpful background on the main characters of Scripture.

The process of spiritual growth is called discipleship. Welcome to the process! As you study, pray, and discuss what you are learning in *Let's Go Deeper*, you are going to gain a deeper knowledge of Jesus, and He is going to change you from the inside out. To make your journey more successful, I have a few suggestions:

Find a good study Bible. You will understand the Scriptures better if you have a modern translation, such as the New American Standard Bible, the New International Version, or the New Living Translation. Older translations, such as the King James Version, are helpful in Bible study, but they are difficult for modern readers to understand. Consider purchasing a study Bible that contains helpful notes at the bottom of each page so you can dig deeper into the Scriptures.

Ask a mentor to help you. Don't try to figure everything out by yourself. The Lord will provide mature Christians who can offer guidance, instruction, and prayer. They will also share the wisdom they've learned over their years of following Jesus. If you have a mentor, ask him or her to do this Bible study with you, and ask for help whenever you have questions.

Join a healthy church. Jesus never intended for us to follow Him in isolation. He invites us into a community where we love and encourage one another. The Bible compares the church to a family. You will grow faster when you allow your Christian fathers, mothers, brothers, and sisters to walk in close fellowship with you. Find a church where the Bible is taught faithfully and where you feel a strong sense of love among the members. This love will provide a healthy place for you to grow.

Make sure you have put your faith in Jesus before you begin. Perhaps as you begin this study you realize you haven't yet made the initial step to follow Jesus. Don't delay that important decision. You can actually make it right now. I encourage you to embrace God's amazing love today and receive the salvation that only Jesus gives. Here are four steps you can take to begin your relationship with God.

1. **Recognize your need.** The Bible tells us that "all have sinned and fall short of the glory of God" (Romans 3:23). All of us are sinners, and we must admit our need for the Savior.

2. **Repent of your sins.** Because God is completely holy and we are sinners, our sins create a wall that separates us from God. By confessing your sins and turning from them, you will find forgiveness. Repent means to make a 180-degree turnaround. The Bible promises, "If we confess our sins, He is faithful and righteous to forgive us our sins and to cleanse us from all unrighteousness" (1 John 1:9).

3. **Believe in Jesus.** God worked a miracle when He sent His only Son to die so that He could pay for all our sins. Put your faith in Him and believe in His power to save you. The Bible says, "For God so loved the world, that He gave His only begotten Son, that whoever believes in Him shall not perish, but have eternal life" (John 3:16).

4. **Receive His salvation.** God has given us this free gift, but we still must accept it. Thank Him for sending Jesus to die on the cross for you. Thank Him for His amazing love, mercy, and forgiveness. Then ask Him to live in your heart. His promise to us is clear: "But as many as received Him, to them He gave the right to become children of God" (John 1:12).

If you have walked through these four steps, you can say this prayer:

Lord Jesus, thank You for dying on the cross for me. I recognize that You are the true Son of God, sent to earth to pay the full price for all our sins. I believe You were raised from the dead and that You live forever in heaven. You are God Almighty, and I submit to Your lordship. I'm sorry that I've lived my life apart from You. Please forgive me for thinking that my life could have true meaning without You, my Creator and Lord.

I turn from my sins and choose to follow You. Please wash me clean and come into my heart. I give You all my hurts, my fears, my unforgiveness, my pride, my greed, and all the garbage of my past. Thank You that I can start my life over again with You. Amen.

The Bible assures us, "If you confess with your mouth Jesus as Lord, and believe in your heart that God raised Him from the dead, you will be saved" (Romans 10:9). If you prayed that prayer, you can have confidence that you have been born again and are now part of God's family. Tell someone else what Jesus has done in your life—and join me in this journey to go deeper in your relationship with Christ!

HEROES OF OUR FAITH

ABRAHAM

He Saw Jesus From Afar

Abraham lived thousands of years ago during a dark time when people worshipped idols. Yet God sought a relationship with this man, who was known as Abram when God first called him to leave the land of Ur (in modern Iraq) to go to a strange land called Canaan—which is now Israel. God told Abram He would give him many descendants so that he would become the founder of a new nation that would honor the true and only God.

Abram struggled to believe God's promise—but ultimately God was pleased with His servant's faith. Abram became known as a "friend of God" (James 2:23). God even changed his name to Abraham, which means "father of a multitude of nations" (Genesis 17:5)—and his children became the pioneers of the Hebrew nation.

The Bible tells us that God revealed to Abraham things that would happen thousands of years later. God commanded Abraham to take his only son, Isaac, and sacrifice him on top of a mountain. Abraham intended to obey the Lord, but God stopped him from killing his son and instead provided a ram for the needed sacrifice. Through this unusual situation, God revealed to Abraham that one day He would sacrifice His own Son, Jesus Christ, to pay for our sins.

Abraham was shown a preview of God's amazing plan of salvation. That's why Galatians 3:8 says, "God...preached the gospel beforehand to Abraham." He must have understood, at least partially, that God would one day forgive His people for their sins. In fact, Jesus said: "Your father Abraham rejoiced to see My day, and he saw it and was glad" (John 8:56). This is why Abraham is called the father of our faith. He was the first person in history to believe that one day the Father would send Jesus to save us.

Perfect and All-Powerful

The Awesome Nature of the True God

"The more I study nature, the more I stand amazed at the work of the Creator."
—LOUIS PASTEUR (1822–1895)
FRENCH CHEMIST AND DISCOVERER OF VACCINES AND PASTEURIZATION

I F YOU SAY the word "God" to a group of people, you will elicit a range of emotions and responses. Some people are adamantly against the idea of any kind of God in the universe. They are *atheists*, and they insist that God is a fictional concept. Other people are *agnostics*, which means they may accept the idea of a God, but they don't believe He cares about people, and they don't think He wants to know us.

Still others believe God is more of a mysterious force that emanates from trees, rocks, animals, and even buildings. And there are *polytheists*—people who believe multiple gods are working behind the scenes to either help or harm people. They believe these gods work mysteriously through stone idols, charms, crystals, mountains, the moon, the stars, or the sun.

But Christians believe there is one true God who sits on the throne of the universe. Even though this God cannot be seen, His glory is obvious in the majesty of His creation, and He kindly invites people to know and worship Him. He shows His kindness to us by sending rain, sunshine, good harvests, and many other blessings. He shows us His beauty and creativity by giving us majestic eagles, fearsome tigers, silly monkeys, frisky puppies, golden leaves in the autumn, flowers in the spring, snowflakes, thunder, delicious fruits, stars in the night sky, more than a million species of insects, and the scents of roses, pine cones, gardenias, and spruce trees.

It's difficult to look at the baffling diversity of creation and not conclude that Someone much smarter than you and me made this earth. Yet there are those who refuse to believe in God because they can't see

1

Him. And many atheists believe that creation, with all its order, wonder, and beauty, just happened by accident.

When we choose to believe in God and serve Him, even though He is invisible, we exercise what the Bible calls *faith*. Hebrews 11:6 explains this by saying:

> And without faith it is impossible to please Him, for he who comes to God must believe that He is and that He is a rewarder of those who seek Him.

This very personal God is also described as the Creator of the entire universe, and He is worthy of all the praise and honor of the world's people. Because He is our Creator and the sustainer of life, He has the right to rule over us and to expect obedience.

In the first chapter of the Bible we read the account of how God created the earth, the galaxies, the sun and moon, the oceans, the atmosphere, and all animal and plant life. We also read that God took special care to create the first people, and He breathed His own breath into them and made them "in His own image" (Genesis 1:27). The story of creation shows us that God desires a special relationship with human beings. He made us so that we could have close fellowship with Him.

The Bible describes God's nature in many other ways:

- He is "God Almighty," which means He has all power (Genesis 17:1).

- He is "eternal," meaning He has existed forever, without a beginning (1 Timothy 1:17).

- He is "immortal," meaning He will have no end (1 Timothy 1:17).

- He is "invisible," meaning He is a spirit (1 Timothy 1:17).

- He is "the only God," which means any other "gods" are unequal to Him (1 Timothy 1:17).

The Bible also says God knows all things (1 John 3:20), He is the source of all wisdom (Proverbs 2:6, CEV), and He is omnipresent (Psalm 33:13–14; 139:7–10)—which means He can be everywhere at one time. God is so great that He has many names. In the Bible He is called "Father," "King,"

"Most High God," "Lord God Almighty," "the Everlasting God," "Judge of all the earth," and many other titles. (See Romans 8:15; 1 Timothy 1:17; Psalm 78:35; Revelation 4:8, MEV; Genesis 21:33; and Genesis 18:25.)

We might assume that extremely intelligent people, such as scientists, would never acknowledge that they believe in God. Yet if you study history you find that some of the most famous scientists were believers. For example, British mathematician Isaac Newton (1643–1727), who laid the foundations of modern physics, said this: "The true God is living, intelligent, and powerful;...he is supreme, or supremely perfect. He is eternal and infinite, omnipotent and omniscient, that is, he endures from eternity to eternity, and he is present from infinity to infinity; he rules all things, and he knows all things that happen or can happen."[1]

We are invited to worship and honor this infinite God, but He doesn't force us to follow Him like robots. He gives us the freedom to choose if we will believe and trust Him. Even though He is lofty and all-powerful, He desires a close, loving relationship with each one of us. This is why 1 John 4:8 says: "God is love."

Thousands of years ago God called a Jewish man named Moses to go to Egypt and liberate the Hebrew slaves from captivity. Moses knew God was real, but he did not know how to identify Him. Moses asked God: "Now they may say to me, 'What is His name?' What shall I say to them?" (Exodus 3:13). God answered: "I AM WHO I AM...thus you shall say to the sons of Israel, 'I AM has sent me to you'" (v. 14). This name, I AM WHO I AM, reveals the nature of our great God. He is all-powerful and eternal; He has always existed, and He always will.

The name I AM WHO I AM is translated "Yahweh" in Hebrew, and later it was sometimes pronounced "Jehovah" in English. It is translated in English as "LORD" more than six thousand times in the Bible. The Hebrew letters used to spell the word Yahweh, YHWH, are three forms of the word meaning "to be." So the word can actually be translated "He was; He is; He will be." So we see that God's name describes His eternal nature. Yahweh also denotes His continuous presence with His people.[2] He is not detached from us. He is not a God who is far away. He is near!

God desires to live among His people in a close relationship. Even though He is almighty and enthroned in the glory of heaven, He makes Himself accessible and available to those who love Him. This all-powerful God stoops low, in amazing humility, so He can help us, save us, forgive us of our sins, comfort us, deliver us, speak to us, and be with us.

In all other religions of the world, God is usually described as detached and uninterested in people; a strict judge with no compassion; or an impersonal, magical force. The true God of the Bible is none of these things. He is a loving, personal Supreme Being who wants to show His incomprehensible love to the people He created in His image. First John 3:1 says God is a good Father who loves His children: "See how great a love the Father has bestowed on us, that we would be called children of God."

The purpose of life is to know and understand God's love for us, and it will actually take eternity for us to comprehend it. God invites us to know Him. He says to us, "You shall love the LORD your God with all your heart and with all your soul and with all your might" (Deuteronomy 6:5). He blesses all who respond to His invitation.

LET'S GO **DEEPER**

What can you learn about God from the following verses?

1. Psalm 103:13

Loving Father to us

2. Psalm 97:9

Supreme over all.

3. Revelation 4:8

God is holy, always ways & shall be.

4. Isaiah 40:28

No one matches to power
He is eternal — he is forever

5. Isaiah 33:22

law giver
The Lord is judge — our King
He is our savior

6. Read 1 Timothy 1:17. What adjectives did the apostle Paul use to describe the nature of God?

Unseen one — never dies

LET'S **TALK** ABOUT IT

What would you say to convince an atheist that there really is a God?

Memory Verse

Worthy are You, our Lord and our God, to receive glory and honor and power; for You created all things, and because of Your will they existed, and were created.

—REVELATION 4:11

HEROES OF OUR FAITH

MOSES

He Handed Down the Law

Before the Father sent Jesus to save us, He had to show us that we could not save ourselves. He called a Jewish man named Moses to leave his comfortable life in Egypt so he could learn God's ways in the wilderness. Moses became closer to God than any person could during those Old Testament times. He saw the glory of God's presence, heard His awesome voice, and obeyed His commands. And God supernaturally used Moses to lead the Jewish people out of slavery in Egypt.

After Moses led the Jews into freedom in the wilderness of the Sinai desert, God gave him His holy Law, along with very detailed plans for how people could approach Him in worship. The Law, which included the Ten Commandments, was incredibly strict, and the regulations for worship required every person to bring animals for sacrifice. Yet these bloody rituals had no real power to cleanse anyone from sin. They were only prophetic previews of how Jesus would one day cleanse us from sin by the shedding of His own blood.

Moses was God's instrument to show people, so long ago, that we need a Savior. Even though Moses was a humble and godly man, he wasn't perfect. No person can be perfect on this side of heaven. Toward the end of his life, Moses got angry and disobeyed one of God's commands, and he was forbidden to enter the Promised Land. His failure reminds us that following a list of rules can't save us. The list simply reminds us of man's need for salvation from our sins.

John 1:17 says: "For the Law was given through Moses; grace and truth were realized through Jesus Christ." Moses reminded us of our sin and God's holiness, but he also pointed us to the only solution—Jesus our Savior.

He's a Tender, Loving Father

The Amazing Character of God

*"We wonder why we don't have faith; the answer is, faith
is confidence in the character of God and if we don't know
what kind of God God is, we can't have faith."*

—A. W. TOZER (1897–1963)
AMERICAN PASTOR AND AUTHOR

EVERY PERSON YOU know has a unique personality and character. Some people are funny. Some are shy and introverted. Some people are warm and sympathetic. Others can be loud and dominant. But what is God like?

His amazing character is described in the Bible in great detail. He is called "good" (Psalm 100:5), "rich in mercy" (Ephesians 2:4–5), "compassionate" (Psalm 103:13, NLT), "a very present help" (Psalm 46:1), "forgiving" (1 John 1:9, NET), "patient toward you" (2 Peter 3:9), "slow to anger" (Psalm 86:15), generous (Philippians 4:19), "faithful" (Lamentations 3:22–23, NLT), "love[s] justice" (Isaiah 61:8), and "holy" (Exodus 15:11, CEV).

"Holy" means He is perfect, with no sin. He is also "strong" (Jeremiah 50:34, NIV), He never gets tired (Isaiah 40:28), He never sleeps (Psalm 121:4), He knows everything about every person He created (Luke 12:7), and He gives His favor and blessing to those who follow and obey Him (Psalm 1:1–3). He also judges wicked people who continue to rebel against Him and harm others. And because He is so protective, He gets angry when people are mistreated, misjudged, or abused.

Who would not want to worship a God like this? Jesus described God this way: "Our Father who is in heaven" (Matthew 6:9). "Father" is the best way for us to understand God. Even though God is perfect, without any flaw, He desires fellowship with the people He created. He pursues a relationship with us. Revelation 3:20 says:

7

> Behold, I stand at the door and knock; if anyone hears My voice
> and opens the door, I will come in to him and will dine with
> him, and he with Me.

When Jesus wanted to paint a picture of the heavenly Father, He
told a story about a Jewish father who had two sons. The younger son
dishonored his family by asking for an early inheritance, leaving his
father's house and going to a foreign country where he wasted all his
money. This is how human beings have treated God. Even though God
blessed us with His goodness, provision, and kindness, we chose to walk
away from it, and we tried to live in total separation from Him. We acted
as though we did not need Him in our lives.

In the story Jesus told, the younger son finally realized his sin, and he
decided to return to his home. He felt very sorry for disappointing his
father. The son also expected the father would punish him, or perhaps
make him work as a servant to pay back the money he squandered.

> When he came to his senses, he said, "How many of my father's
> hired men have more than enough bread, but I am dying here
> with hunger! I will get up and go to my father, and will say to
> him, 'Father, I have sinned against heaven, and in your sight; I
> am no longer worthy to be called your son; make me as one of
> your hired men.'"
>
> —LUKE 15:17–19

Amazingly, the father in Jesus' story wasn't angry. He didn't disown his
son for his dishonorable behavior or send him out in the fields to repay
his debt. The father was prayerfully looking down the road, waiting for
his son to return! When the father saw his wayward son walking toward
the house, he ran to him with open arms, embraced him, kissed him,
and welcomed him back home.

> The father said to his slaves, "Quickly bring out the best robe and
> put it on him, and put a ring on his hand and sandals on his feet;
> and bring the fattened calf, kill it, and let us eat and celebrate; for
> this son of mine was dead and has come to life again; he was lost
> and has been found." And they began to celebrate.
>
> —LUKE 15:22–24

The father showed unconditional love to his son, even though he could have banished him from the family property and cut him out of his life forever. The good father invited his beloved son back into his house, gave him a robe, and even threw a party for him. (See Luke 15:11–32.)

There is a famous painting of this story called *The Return of the Prodigal Son* by eighteenth-century Italian artist Pompeo Batoni. It shows the father lovingly covering his son with his bright red robe. Jesus didn't mention the color of the robe in His parable—He simply called it the "best robe." But the painter made it red to remind us that our Father, in His abounding mercy, covers us with the blood of Jesus so we can live in His house forever.

God has many amazing qualities, but His merciful love for us is His greatest characteristic. God invites us to return to Him, no matter how sinful we have been. He is not angry at us—He waits on His front porch, looking down the road with hopes that we will leave our sin, repent, and return to Him. And even though He is perfect, He forgives our sins so we can experience His love. When you decided to follow the good Father, He ran to you, embraced you, and threw a lavish party to celebrate your homecoming.

LET'S GO **DEEPER**

1. Psalm 139:13–16 says God knows everything about us, yet He loves us in spite of our flaws and mistakes. Read this passage. If God is your Creator, what should be your response to Him?

_____

_____

_____

2. Read Psalm 86:15. How is God's character described in this passage?

_____

_____

_____

3. Read the story of the good father and the prodigal son in Luke 15:11–32. How would you describe God from this story?

_____

_____

_____

4. The apostle Paul said our goal in life is "to know the love of Christ which surpasses knowledge" (Ephesians 3:19). What have you learned about God from this lesson?

_____

_____

_____

LET'S **TALK** ABOUT IT

Before you became a Christian, how did you view God? How have your views of God changed since then?

Memory Verse

Who is a God like you, pardoning iniquity and passing over transgression for the remnant of his inheritance? He does not retain his anger forever, because he delights in steadfast love. He will again have compassion on us; he will tread our iniquities underfoot. You will cast all our sins into the depths of the sea.

—MICAH 7:18–19, ESV

HEROES OF OUR FAITH

PAUL

Apostle to the Gentiles

The apostle Paul is considered the bravest and strongest Christian of the New Testament period, but he didn't start out as a follower of Jesus. In his early career as a Jewish Pharisee, Paul hated Christians and tried to obliterate the new religion. But after the resurrected Jesus appeared to him during a journey to Syria, Paul had a dramatic, darkness-to-light conversion and became a bold apologist for the Christian faith. In many ways he was a spiritual father to the movement, not only because of his deep spiritual insights but also because of his intense love for people.

Paul's legacy was preserved for us through his writings. Thirteen of his very personal letters to churches in Rome, Corinth, Ephesus, Colossae, and other cities make up more than 30 percent of the New Testament, and they provide a deep revelation of who Jesus is and what He did for us. But Paul was not a brainy theologian living in an ivory tower; he trekked across mountains and crossed oceans to carry the gospel, and he suffered greatly for his faith. He also wrote many of his letters from prison. During his dangerous missionary trips to Asia Minor, Greece, and Italy, he was beaten, stoned, shipwrecked, snake-bitten, deprived of food and sleep, and falsely accused. Yet he wrote to the Romans: "If God is for us, who can be against us?" (Romans 8:31, NIV).

One of Paul's greatest accomplishments was helping the first churches shift from being Jewish only to being inclusive of all races and nationalities. Many early Christians came from a Jewish background and had disdain for non-Jews; Paul carried a revolutionary message of unity, teaching that Jesus had broken down the wall that separated Jews from Gentiles. He bravely declared: "There is neither Jew nor Greek, there is neither slave nor free man, there is neither male nor female; for you are all one in Christ Jesus" (Galatians 3:28). Paul spent the last years of his life encouraging the churches that were spreading fast all over the Roman Empire, but he paid dearly for his devotion—he was executed by the Roman emperor Nero. The words the Holy Spirit inspired Paul to write provide a solid spiritual foundation for us today.

Father, Son, and Holy Spirit

The Wondrous Mystery of the Trinity

"Bring me a worm that can comprehend a man, and then I will
show you a man that can comprehend the triune God."

—JOHN WESLEY (1703–1791)
BRITISH EVANGELIST AND FOUNDER OF METHODISM

THE BIBLE DESCRIBES God as a "triune" being—that means He is three in one. God is Father, Son, and Holy Spirit. The apostle Peter used this three-in-one language when he wrote: "To God's elect...who have been chosen according to the foreknowledge of *God the Father*, through the sanctifying work of *the Spirit*, to be obedient to *Jesus Christ* and sprinkled with his blood" (1 Peter 1:1–2, NIV, emphasis added).

New Testament writers made it clear that each member of the Trinity is God. All three are fully and unequivocally God. Yet they never operate apart from each other. The Father, Son, and Holy Spirit flow in an inexplicable harmony.

After the New Testament was written, early Christian leaders wrote summary statements, called creeds, that explained this difficult concept of a Trinity to people who were used to worshipping hundreds of pagan idols. One of the most well-known of these is the Nicene Creed, written in AD 325. It says (emphasis added):

> I believe in one God, the *Father* almighty, maker of heaven and earth, of all things visible and invisible. I believe in one Lord *Jesus Christ*, the Only Begotten Son of God, born of the Father before all ages....I believe in the *Holy Spirit*, the Lord, the giver of life, who proceeds from the Father and the Son, who with the Father and the Son is adored and glorified, who has spoken through the prophets.[1]

The concept of the Trinity appears in the very first chapter of the Bible. After God created the earth, the seas, and the animals, He said: "Let us make mankind in our image, in our likeness" (Genesis 1:26). Who is "us"? Why did God refer to Himself in the plural? This is a reference to the Father, Son, and Holy Spirit. The triune God has existed forever. The Son was with the Father at creation, and Genesis 1:2 says the Holy Spirit was also involved in creation from the beginning.

In his masterpiece *Mere Christianity*, British author C. S. Lewis attempts to explain the Trinity in human terms while acknowledging that this is quite impossible because we don't live in the same realm God does. Lewis describes the realm of human beings as one-dimensional and God's realm as a three-dimensional universe. He writes:

> In God's dimension, so to speak, you find a being who is three Persons while remaining one Being, just as a cube is six squares while remaining one cube. Of course we cannot fully conceive a Being like that: just as, if we were so made that we perceived only two dimensions in space we could never properly imagine a cube. But we can get a sort of faint notion of it. And when we do, we are then, for the first time in our lives, getting some positive idea, however faint, of something super-personal—something more than a person. It is something we could never have guessed, and yet, once we have been told, one almost feels one ought to have been able to guess it because it fits in so well with all the things we know already.[2]

If the idea of a Trinity was "faint" to C. S. Lewis, a brainy intellectual who lectured at both Oxford and Cambridge in England, how much more difficult is it for the common person to grasp? How do we explain to unbelievers that the God we worship is a Trinity? We must understand three simple truths: (1) there is only one God; (2) the Father, Son, and Holy Spirit are three distinct persons; and (3) each of these persons is fully God.

The triune nature of God is spelled out in the Old Testament. But the Trinity is more clearly defined in the New Testament, even though the actual word *Trinity* never appears in Scripture. It is clearest in the passage where Jesus gives us His final Great Commission in Matthew 28:18–19: "All authority has been given to Me in heaven and on earth. Go therefore and make disciples of all the nations, baptizing them in the name of the *Father* and the *Son* and the *Holy Spirit*" (emphasis added). It is interesting that the Greek word for "name" in this passage is singular. The name is one, yet three persons are mentioned!

When Jesus is baptized by John the Baptist in Mark 1:10–11, we see the Trinity on full display. In this scene, the Father declares His audible blessing over the Son, and the Holy Spirit descends on the Son in the form of a dove. The Father, Son, and Spirit are revealed together. This shows us that Father, Son, and Spirit have their own unique identities—the Father is not the Son; the Son is not the Spirit; the Spirit is not the Father. They are distinct persons, and yet they enjoy a unity that is, for us mortals, incomprehensible.

What is most beautiful about the Trinity is that all true Christians are invited into close, intimate fellowship with all three persons of the Godhead. You can have fellowship with the Father, the Son, and the Holy Spirit.

How can God be three and one at the same time? Author A. W. Tozer wrote: "To meditate on the three Persons of the Godhead is to walk in thought through the garden eastward in Eden and to tread on holy ground. Our sincerest effort to grasp the incomprehensible mystery of the Trinity must remain forever futile, and only by deepest reverence can it be saved from actual presumption."[3]

But this complexity of the Trinity should not discourage us. Rather it shows us that God is not on our level. His ways are so much higher than ours.

That is why we worship Him! He is high and exalted above everything on earth. We worship Him not only because of His great love, mercy, and perfection but because He is so incredibly wondrous that we cannot fully understand Him. We simply stand with our jaws dropped in amazement and praise Him for who He is!

LET'S GO **DEEPER**

The following verses mention the triune God. Read each passage and write down how the three members of the Trinity are described.

1. Luke 3:22

_____

_____

_____

2. Galatians 4:6

_____

_____

_____

3. John 15:26

_____

_____

_____

4. Acts 10:38

_____

_____

_____

5. 1 Peter 1:2

_____

_____

_____

LET'S **TALK** ABOUT IT

How would you explain the triune nature of God to someone who isn't familiar with the Christian faith?

Memory Verse

Go therefore and make disciples of all the nations, baptizing them in the name of the Father and the Son and the Holy Spirit.

—MATTHEW 28:19

HEROES OF OUR FAITH

ISAIAH

He Saw Jesus on His Throne

The prophet Isaiah lived seven hundred years before Christ, during a very chaotic time in Israel's history. But God revealed His wonderful plan of redemption to Isaiah so that he made many prophecies about the coming of Jesus. Isaiah's message alone should convince people that God is real. There are at least nineteen very specific prophecies about the coming of Jesus in the writings of Isaiah.

For example, Isaiah prophesied that Jesus would be born of a virgin (Isaiah 7:14); He would preach in Galilee (9:1-2); He would be heir in the lineage of David (9:6-7); He would heal blind, deaf, poor, and needy people (29:18-19); His persecutors would spit on Him and strike Him (50:6); He would bear our sins in His body (53:4); He would be buried in a rich man's tomb (53:9); and the Gentiles would one day seek Him (11:10).

How could Isaiah predict all these details so accurately when he lived so many centuries before Christ? The answer is in Isaiah 6, where we read that the prophet had a powerful encounter with God. He saw a vision of the throne room of heaven, where the Son of God was seated in all His glory. Isaiah cried out: "For my eyes have seen the King, the LORD of hosts" (Isaiah 6:5). In that holy place, Isaiah got a preview of what was coming. He saw Jesus and understood His global mission to cleanse and redeem mankind. This is why the apostle John wrote in his Gospel that Isaiah saw the glory of Jesus (John 12:41). Isaiah's vision of the Savior empowered him to preach about Jesus hundreds of years before His coming.

Lost in Total Darkness

The Problem of Man's Sinfulness

"Sin is in our heart; we love that which is evil….Like a sea which comes up and floods a continent, penetrating every valley, deluging every plain, and invading every mountain, so has sin penetrated our entire nature."

—CHARLES H. SPURGEON (1834-1892)
BRITISH PREACHER AND AUTHOR

GOD DIDN'T CREATE human beings to be sinners. When He made the first man and woman—Adam and Eve—God wanted them to enjoy fellowship with Him forever. He created them to enjoy life forever, and He authorized them to rule over the earth. But the man and woman disobeyed God and through their actions brought the whole earth under the control of sin. Their tragic decision also brought sickness, pain, grief, poverty, perversion, and every other form of evil into the world. The result of all this sin was physical and spiritual death.

Often you will hear people say, "I believe people are basically good," but this is not a biblical concept. Ecclesiastes 7:20 says, "Indeed, there is not a righteous man on earth who continually does good and who never sins." Through the original sins of Adam and Eve, mankind became "depraved"—which means morally corrupt and wicked. This explains why our world is so full of crime, violence, hatred, war, family conflict, injustice, racism, child abuse, and so many other social ills. The human race is infected with an incurable sickness called sin.

People can try to put on a mask of moral behavior, but the Bible says all people are hopelessly trapped in a sinful condition. We are not "basically good." Jeremiah 17:9 says: "The heart is more deceitful than all else and is desperately sick; who can understand it?" And Romans 3:23 says, "All have sinned and fall short of the glory of God." The Bible even says that we are "slaves of corruption" (2 Peter 2:19)—which means we cannot help ourselves from doing wrong things. Because of our sinful nature, all human beings deserve to be eternally separated from God.

Throughout the Bible we see evidence of the total sinfulness of human beings. Theologians have called this condition "total depravity." We sometimes are tempted to minimize the wickedness of sin by saying such things as, "She has a good heart," or the famous, "The devil made him do it." But the Bible is clear that we sin because we want to sin. It is our nature. British preacher Charles Spurgeon once said, "As the salt flavors every drop of the Atlantic, so does sin affect every atom of our nature. It is so sadly there, so abundantly there, that if you cannot detect it you are deceived."[1]

Many centuries ago God gave the people of Israel His Law to show them, and us, how far we fall short of His perfection. When God gave Moses the Ten Commandments, recorded in Exodus 20:1–17, the people understood that sinful man has offended God through idolatry (worshipping other gods), disrespecting God, dishonoring parents, murder, adultery, stealing, lying, and coveting, among other things.

The Bible also says God is angry at sinful men because they have rebelled against His wise and loving authority. Romans 1:18 says: "For the wrath of God is revealed from heaven against all ungodliness and unrighteousness of men who suppress the truth in unrighteousness." God has a legal right to be angry with sinful people because they have broken His laws. Because of our sin, we deserve death. God could have decided to destroy us all. Yet because He is so loving, He made a legal way to forgive us and deliver us from the punishment we deserve.

During earth's early history, the world became so corrupted by evil that God decided to destroy it with a flood. He had every right to do this because man had foolishly rebelled against God's authority. Yet in that moment God's mercy became evident. He showed favor to one man, Noah, and commanded him to build a huge boat that could preserve his family as well as all species of animals. Those who hid inside Noah's ark were saved from God's judgment. God provided a way of escape.

Sometime in the future God will once again bring judgment on all those who choose sin and reject Him. But until then all sinners have been given the opportunity to be saved from final destruction. But this time, instead of hiding in a giant boat, all we have to do is put our trust in Jesus and hide in His love and mercy. He is our ark of safety. And when we believe in Christ, He forgives our sin and gives us grace to live the way God intended. This is the miracle of forgiveness!

LET'S GO **DEEPER**

1. List the many ways Romans 1:28–32 says human beings sin against God.

_____

_____

What do the following verses say about the sinfulness of man?

2. Genesis 6:5

_____

3. Isaiah 53:6

_____

4. Read Psalm 14:2–3. What did God see when He looked down at human beings on earth?

_____

LET'S **TALK** ABOUT IT

When you look around at the world today, what evidence do you see that the whole world is in total bondage to sin?

Memory Verse

If we say that we have no sin, we are deceiving ourselves and the truth is not in us.

—1 JOHN 1:8

HEROES OF OUR FAITH

LUKE

The Good Doctor

We know little about Luke's background, yet this gifted historian wrote more than one-fourth of the New Testament. He was most likely a Gentile, which is perhaps why he made such a good traveling companion for the apostle Paul during their journeys to Asia Minor, Greece, and Rome. We are indebted to this meticulous researcher because he carefully interviewed the eyewitnesses of Jesus' life, death, and resurrection. We aren't sure if Luke ever met Jesus personally, but he talked extensively to those who did and recorded their stories for us.

Luke's Gospel shines a unique light on the humanity of Jesus. It gives us a full report on the Savior's birth, and it is the only Gospel to give any detail about Jesus' childhood. Many scholars believe Luke must have interviewed Mary, the mother of Jesus, to learn so many important facts. Luke's Gospel is also the only one that gives details about the women who followed Jesus (Luke 8:1-3), so he probably interviewed them too, along with hundreds of other people who walked and talked with Jesus and saw Him after His resurrection.

Described by Paul as "the beloved physician" (Colossians 4:14), Luke must have been a compassionate man who cared for others, including his friend Paul, who struggled with some unspecified ailments. Luke was a part of Paul's missionary journeys. He saw Paul cast out a demon from a slave girl in Philippi; he was there when Paul said farewell to the church elders in Ephesus; he was on the ship when the entire crew almost died on the voyage to Rome. Luke is the only Gospel writer to tell us about the heavenly flames that came upon the early disciples on the day of Pentecost. That same flame of the Holy Spirit inspired him to write the official record of the first-century church.

What a Glorious Savior

Who Is Jesus Christ?

"There are many wells today, but they are dry. There are many hungry souls today that are empty. But let us come to Jesus and take Him at His Word and we will find wells of salvation, and be able to draw waters out of the well of salvation, for Jesus is that well."

—WILLIAM J. SEYMOUR (1870–1922)
AFRICAN AMERICAN PREACHER AND PENTECOSTAL PIONEER

HOLLYWOOD HAS ALWAYS struggled to give an accurate depiction of Jesus Christ on film. Even though the historic Jesus was a Jewish man from ancient Israel who spoke Aramaic and Hebrew, He has often been portrayed as a White guy with a British accent, as He was in movies such as *King of Kings* (1961) and *The Greatest Story Ever Told* (1965).

There will probably never be a movie that represents Jesus with total accuracy, since we have no photographs of Him. But what we do have, in the Bible, is a complex, four-dimensional portrait of Him in words, written by people who were eyewitnesses of who He was and what He did.

We have four very different accounts of His life on earth, written by four different men who received their words from the Holy Spirit. As you begin your journey of faith, one of the first things you should do is read all four of these Gospels: Matthew, Mark, Luke, and John. They will give you a 360-degree perspective of the most amazing person who ever lived.

It is important for you to study all four Gospels so you can get an accurate picture of Jesus from all angles.

The Gospel of Matthew reveals Jesus as the long-awaited Messiah who was promised to the Jewish people. Matthew was a Jew, and he wrote his Gospel to Jews to prove that Jesus was the Savior promised by the Old Testament prophets. Matthew's Gospel contains a genealogy that shows how Joseph, Jesus' adoptive Jewish father, was the descendant of Abraham, the father of the Jewish nation.

Matthew structures his Gospel around five sermons of Jesus, reminding us of the Torah, the first five books of the Old Testament, written by Moses. By writing his Gospel in this way, Matthew was showing Jewish people that Jesus was greater than Moses, who was revered as the great Jewish lawgiver. The Gospel of Matthew contains more quotes from the Old Testament than any other Gospel, in order to prove that Isaiah, Jeremiah, Hosea, Micah, and all the revered Jewish prophets saw Jesus from a distance and spoke of Him.

The Gospel of Mark was written by a Jewish man, but it is addressed to non-Jewish people who did not care much about Old Testament prophecies. Mark's Gospel focuses on the mighty works of Jesus rather than His teachings. In fact, it records more miracles than any other Gospel. It shows us Jesus healing the sick, opening blind eyes, cleansing lepers, raising the dead, calming storms, and multiplying food for hungry crowds. In Mark we see Jesus as a powerful Savior who conquered sin, sickness, and death. Bible scholars believe that Mark wrote his Gospel based on the experiences of Peter, who was one of Jesus' closest disciples. In fact, Mark is written from Peter's unique vantage point.

The Gospel of Luke was written by a Gentile for Gentiles who didn't know much about the Jewish faith. It focuses on the humanity of Jesus—proving that Jesus was not only fully God but fully human. It contains a detailed description of Jesus' birth, reminding us that Jesus was supernaturally conceived by a virgin, Mary. It is the only Gospel that shows us a scene from Jesus' childhood, reminding us that He grew up in a human family and experienced normal human struggles. And the genealogy of Jesus in Luke's Gospel traces Jesus' lineage from Adam, the father of all mankind, to Mary, Jesus' mother. It proves to us that Jesus was God in human flesh. Luke's Gospel also focuses on how compassionate Jesus was toward human suffering.

The Gospel of John was written by a Jew, but his audience is the world. It boldly describes Jesus as the Son of God and focuses on the fact that He was fully God in the flesh. Unlike all the other Gospels, John's opens with a reference to the creation of the world in Genesis and shows that Jesus was with the Father at the moment of creation.

John's Gospel shows us that Jesus is God. In the Old Testament God was revealed as "Jehovah," or "I AM." In John, Jesus uses seven "I ams" to describe Himself. He said:

- "I am the bread of life" (John 6:35).

- "I am the Light of the world" (John 8:12).

- "I am the door" (John 10:7).

- "I am the good shepherd" (John 10:11).

- "I am the resurrection and the life" (John 11:25).

- "I am the way, and the truth, and the life" (John 14:6).

- "I am the true vine" (John 15:1).

These "I am" passages all reveal that Jesus is one with the God of the Old Testament. He came to earth to show us who the Father is.

When we read all four Gospels, along with other writings about Him in the Old and New Testaments, we get a widescreen view of this amazing Savior. It is almost impossible to describe Him because of His greatness. That is why the apostle Paul, one of the great pioneers of early Christian faith, described Jesus as "unfathomable" in Ephesians 3:8. But let us attempt to summarize what we know about Jesus Christ:

- He existed with God before the creation of the world.

- Many Old Testament prophets predicted that He would come to earth as God's "Anointed One," or "Messiah."

- He was born to earthly parents, Joseph and Mary, in Judea, but they knew that He was the Son of God because He was conceived by the Holy Spirit.

- When Jesus was thirty years old He began to preach about God's love and forgiveness to the people of Israel, and for three and a half years He performed many amazing miracles to prove He was the Messiah.

- Jesus was both fully God and fully man so He could be the perfect, sinless sacrifice to pay for our sins. This is why John the Baptist called Jesus "the Lamb of God" (John 1:29); he knew Jesus would be sacrificed to atone for our sins.

- Jesus was arrested and crucified by Roman soldiers in Jerusalem, buried in a tomb, and then raised from the dead after three days.

- About five hundred of Jesus' followers saw Him after He was resurrected, and they began to tell everyone about Him.

- After His resurrection Jesus ascended to heaven and sat down at the right hand of the Father, where He is seated today as King of the universe.

The Christian life is really a journey of getting to know this amazing Son of God. In fact, Jesus Himself told us that knowing Him is the essence of life itself. He said in John 17:3: "This is eternal life, that they may know You, the only true God, and Jesus Christ whom You have sent." Growing in your faith is not just about accumulating knowledge about God—it is cultivating an intimate relationship with Him.

LET'S GO **DEEPER**

1. When the angel spoke to Mary about the coming of Jesus, how did he describe Jesus' mission on earth in Matthew 1:21?

_____

2. In Acts 10:38, in a sermon by the apostle Peter, how is Jesus described?

_____

_____

_____

3. Why did Jesus come to earth, according to 1 John 4:14?

_____

4. In 1 Timothy 2:5, how is Jesus described, and what does this mean?

_____

5. What did Jesus do for us, according to 2 Timothy 1:10?

_____

6. What two titles are given to Jesus Christ, according to Acts 2:36?

_____

7. What name is inscribed on the resurrected Jesus in Revelation 19:16?

_____

When the apostle Paul wrote about the triumphant Jesus Christ who paid for our sins and conquered death, he said in Colossians 1:17–18: "He is before all things, and in Him all things hold together. He is also head of the body, the church; and He is the beginning, the firstborn from the dead, so that He Himself will come to have first place in everything."

Paul teaches us here that Christ is *preeminent,* or surpassing all others. He is the supreme God and the Lord of all the earth. No other god can save us. He is the only way to salvation. He deserves our obedience because He is the true God, and we should humbly submit to His loving authority because the Father has crowned the Son with all glory and honor. Jesus was not just a good teacher; He was not just a Savior. He is both Lord and Savior. We owe Him our full allegiance!

LET'S **TALK** ABOUT IT

Jesus said He is the only way to the Father. How would you explain this to someone who believes that all religions lead to God?

Memory Verse

Jesus said to him, "I am the way, and the truth, and the life; no one comes to the Father but through Me."

—JOHN 14:6

HEROES OF OUR FAITH

MARY, THE MOTHER OF JESUS

She Gave Birth to the Savior

It's ironic that some Christians began elevating Jesus' mother, Mary, to almost godlike status during the early centuries of the church, because this woman was a humble servant who didn't want that kind of attention. We know most about her from Luke's Gospel. This young Jewish woman from Nazareth was visited by an angel, who told her that she would be supernaturally impregnated by the Holy Spirit and give birth to God's Son. God chose her to bring the Messiah into the world.

When Mary learned this news she replied to the angel, "Behold, the bondslave of the Lord; may it be done to me according to your word" (Luke 1:38). Her obedience was costly. She and her husband, Joseph, raised Jesus in typical Jewish fashion, yet she knew He was different and that His path would not be easy. When Jesus began His ministry, Mary and Jesus' other siblings were not supportive at first; perhaps Mary was simply being a protective mother.

Mary certainly didn't want to see her son suffering, yet that is exactly what happened. When she watched Jesus die on the cross, she most likely recalled what the angel told her husband in a dream: "You shall call His name Jesus, for He will save His people from their sins" (Matthew 1:21). As Mary listened to her son's agonizing cries at Calvary, she knew He had paid for the sins of the whole world.

An estimated five hundred of Jesus' followers saw Him after His resurrection. But no one had a closer view of Him than Mary. She carried Him in her womb for nine months, bathed and nursed Him as an infant, marveled at His spiritual insights when He was a growing boy, witnessed His first miracle at the wedding in Cana, and wept as He was crucified. She prayed for the outpouring of the Holy Spirit at Pentecost; she was part of the early church in Jerusalem, and tradition suggests she later moved to Ephesus with the apostle John, who took care of her in her old age. Mary did not want to be worshipped, and her attitude of full surrender to God is unmatched.

LESSON 6

The Incarnation Miracle

How Jesus Is Both God and Man

"The Almighty appeared on earth as a helpless human baby, needing to be fed and changed and taught to talk like any other child. The more you think about it, the more staggering it gets. Nothing in fiction is so fantastic as this truth of the Incarnation."

—J. I. PACKER (1926-2020)
CANADIAN PASTOR, THEOLOGIAN, AND AUTHOR

MILLIONS OF PEOPLE around the world celebrate Christmas every year—including a lot of people who aren't Christians. They enjoy holiday songs and traditions but they actually have only a vague idea of what the original Christmas celebration is all about. But if you explore history, you'll learn that early Christians honored Christmas to commemorate the birth of Jesus in ancient Israel.

The birth of Jesus is certainly worthy of a global holiday, because His coming to this earth was surrounded by special miracles recorded in Scripture. First, ancient prophets foretold that Jesus would be born in the town of Bethlehem in Israel and that He would be called "Immanuel" (Isaiah 7:14), which means "God with us."

An angel told Jesus' mother, Mary, that she would have a child even though she was a virgin. When the holy child arrived, a multitude of angels appeared in fields in Bethlehem to celebrate His birth. And a huge star appeared over Jesus' birthplace as a heavenly signal that the Messiah had arrived to be the true Light of the world.

But how did Jesus, the Son of God, leave heaven to become a man on earth? This happened through what Christians call the *incarnation*. God became human flesh through the miracle of the virgin birth. When the time came for Jesus to come to earth, the angel Gabriel told Mary (who was probably a teenager at the time) that she would become the mother

29

of the Messiah. Then the Holy Spirit caused Mary to become pregnant, even though she had not been with a man.

With God as His father and a young Jewish woman as His mother, Jesus was both fully God and fully man. The Gospel of John states this truth plainly:

> And the Word became flesh, and dwelt among us, and we saw His glory, glory as of the only begotten from the Father, full of grace and truth.
>
> —JOHN 1:14

This phrase "dwelt among us" means, in the Greek language, "tabernacle" or to live temporarily.[1] Jesus preexisted with the Father in heaven, but then He came to earth and was born as a baby and lived in a human body until it was time for Him to sacrifice His life for us. The incarnation is perhaps the greatest miracle of the Christian faith.

Secularists and atheists have mocked the virgin birth for centuries. Thomas Jefferson called it a fable.[2] The concept of a woman giving birth to a baby without a man's involvement is ludicrous to unbelievers. It contradicts all the laws of biology.

Yet Jesus' mother was not a scoffer. When she asked the angel how she would bear this child, he said: "The Holy Spirit will come upon you, and the power of the Most High will overshadow you" (Luke 1:35). The word *overshadow* means "to envelop in a haze of brilliancy."[3] The conception of Christ was obviously an inexplicable miracle!

Mary believed Gabriel's announcement and submitted to God in childlike faith. The incarnation of Jesus cannot be explained in purely scientific terms. There was nothing sexual about it, yet Mary became pregnant without Joseph's sperm. God became human flesh. Divinity put on humanity, and Jesus began a nine-month gestation in Mary's womb.

The virgin birth is not a trivial detail in the story of Jesus. It is a cornerstone of our faith. If it didn't happen, Jesus wouldn't be the Son of God. Everything we believe about salvation would be false if Jesus hadn't been divinely conceived.

When Jesus was born, there was a normal amount of blood, sweat, and tears—because Mary was a human in the painful process of labor. But this birth was surrounded with wonder because Joseph was not the father. Joseph came from a line of Jewish kings, but his pedigree was not enough to save the human race. Joseph could not contribute to this miracle. Bible teacher R. T. Kendall put it this way: "The virgin birth of Christ shows that salvation can never come through human effort."[4] God did this miracle without man's help.

In the early centuries of the church, many people struggled to understand the complexity of the incarnation. So some church leaders got together and wrote a clear statement to help people understand this truth. The Nicene Creed, written in AD 325, says this in part:

> We believe in one Lord, Jesus Christ, the only Son of God, eternally begotten of the Father, God from God, Light from Light, true God from true God, begotten, not made, of one Being with the Father. Through Him all things were made. For us and for our salvation He came down from heaven: by the power of the Holy Spirit He became incarnate from the Virgin Mary, and was made man.[5]

The miraculous incarnation of Jesus is a key cornerstone in our Christian faith. Doubters suggest Joseph got Mary pregnant out of wedlock. But if that were true, Christianity itself would be a lie because (1) if Jesus were not born of a woman, He could not have identified with our sins fully; and (2) if God were not His biological father, Jesus could not have redeemed us. By the power of the Holy Spirit, God became man.

LET'S GO **DEEPER**

1. Read Isaiah 7:14. What did the ancient prophet Isaiah predict would happen?

_____

_____

_____

2. Read Matthew 1:20–21. After Mary became pregnant with Jesus, her fiancé, Joseph, was planning to end the engagement because it looked as if Mary were in disgrace. But then an angel appeared to Joseph in a dream and told him to wed Mary. What did the angel say about Jesus?

_____

_____

_____

3. Isaiah gave another prophecy about the coming Messiah in Isaiah 9:6. How is Jesus described in this verse?

_____

_____

_____

4. Read Philippians 2:5–7. Although Jesus existed in the form of God, what did He then do?

_____

_____

_____

5. Read Colossians 2:9–10. What does it mean when Paul says that in Jesus "all the fullness of Deity dwells in bodily form"? Why is it so important that Jesus was both fully man and fully God?

_____

_____

_____

LET'S **TALK** ABOUT IT

In your own words, explain why it was so important for Jesus to be born of a virgin.

Memory Verse

Being found in appearance as a man, He humbled Himself by becoming obedient to the point of death, even death on a cross.

—PHILIPPIANS 2:8

HEROES OF OUR FAITH

DAVID

The Greatest Worship Leader

David was a wise king, a brave warrior, and a loyal friend, but most of all he is known for being a skilled musician and passionate worshipper. He wrote at least seventy-three of the psalms in the Bible, and in them we catch a glimpse of how he loved to sing, raise his hands, shout wildly, and even dance exuberantly before the Lord. Even though he lived more than two thousand years before Christ, he remains today a role model for all those who love the true God.

David was also a prophet. In Psalm 22 he accurately predicted the sufferings Jesus would experience on the cross. David spoke about Jesus' agony during the crucifixion, His thirst while on the cross, the fierce taunts He received from those who watched His execution, and the casting of lots for His garments. Under the anointing of the Holy Spirit, David also wrote: "A band of evildoers has encompassed me; they pierced my hands and my feet" (Psalm 22:16). Amazingly, Jesus recited this psalm while Roman soldiers nailed His hands and feet to a crude wooden cross. When Jesus said, "It is finished," at the moment of His death, He was quoting the last verse of Psalm 22, "He has done it!" (NIV).

David was known as "a man after [God's] own heart" (1 Samuel 13:14). He rose early in the morning to praise the Lord; he poured out his heart in prayer; he often spoke of his hunger and thirst for God. He experienced many crushing defeats and struggled with his own sin, but his failures drove him closer to God, and he experienced the Lord's forgiveness. He wrote in Psalm 51:2–3, "Wash me thoroughly from my iniquity and cleanse me from my sin. For I know my transgressions." David taught us that we cannot experience true worship if we don't understand God's amazing forgiveness.

LESSON 7

The Greatest Moment in History

How Jesus Saved Us on the Cross

"God proved His love on the Cross. When Christ hung, and
bled, and died, it was God saying to the world, 'I love you.'"
—BILLY GRAHAM (1918–2018)
AMERICAN EVANGELIST

IMAGINE IF THE police arrested you for selling drugs. You would be booked into jail, and eventually you would stand before a judge who would declare the seriousness of your crime. Then you would have your day in court.

A lawyer might defend you, but a jury would listen to a description of your crimes. And most likely the jury would rule that you were guilty after listening to witnesses who saw you breaking the law. The judge would announce to everyone in the courtroom that you were guilty of drug dealing. And then you would be sentenced to several years in prison. In fact, you might never get out.

But also imagine that on the day of your sentencing, the judge announced that you had been pardoned. Imagine him saying: "Even though you are guilty, I have decided to remove all record of wrongs from your files. You are innocent." This rarely happens in a court of law. But this is what happened when Jesus chose to forgive us for our sins. He freed us from all charges. He removed the stain of guilt. And He announced that instead of us being sinful, we are now righteous.

This is what we call the miracle of redemption. Redemption means "the ransom or deliverance of sinners from the bondage of sin and the penalties of God's violated law by the atonement of Christ."[1] When Jesus chose to die for us, even when we were sinners, He set us free from all the punishment we deserved. We will spend the rest of eternity thanking God for this miracle!

But how did Jesus do this? God is just, so He couldn't arbitrarily change His own law. Sin has to be punished. He did it by transferring the sins of the world to Jesus, along with all the guilt and shame. This is what happened when Jesus was crucified.

In the Old Testament, before Jesus came to the world, God showed us that He would send a Savior to pay for our sins. He gave the Jewish people an elaborate system of animal sacrifice. During those days, a faithful follower of God had to take a lamb, a goat, or a bird to the tabernacle and give it to the priest, and the priest would kill it on God's altar. Of course, we know the blood of an innocent lamb cannot really pay for a person's sins, but God used this vivid illustration to teach people what was coming. God was showing us that one day He would send a perfect sacrifice to pay the debt we owed for our sins.

When Jesus began His ministry in Israel, the prophet John the Baptist saw Him and declared: "Behold, the Lamb of God who takes away the sin of the world!" (John 1:29). Jesus was the perfect Lamb. Because He lived a sinless life, He was able to perform this amazing transaction. It was the ultimate act of mercy and selfless love.

When Jesus was crucified on the cross, God put all the sins of the whole world on His Son. Jesus died in our place. He took our guilt. And because Jesus was willing to die for us, all our sins have been forgiven. We do not have to work to obtain this forgiveness! All we have to do is believe in Jesus and accept the free gift of His mercy. Titus 3:5 says, "He saved us, not on the basis of deeds which we have done in righteousness, but according to His mercy, by the washing of regeneration and renewing by the Holy Spirit."

It's important for us to understand the horrible death that Jesus endured for us. Nobody performed an autopsy on Jesus' mangled body after He was crucified. But doctors who have studied the Bible's description of His death say the pain would have been beyond excruciating. In fact, the word *excruciating* means "out of the cross."[2] Jesus literally defined the worst pain anyone could feel.

His suffering began in a garden called Gethsemane, where God laid the sins of the world on His beloved Son. Hebrews 5:7 says Jesus offered up prayers "with loud crying and tears" during this moment of anguish. Luke's Gospel says the agony was so strong that Jesus' sweat "became like drops of blood, falling down upon the ground" (Luke 22:44). The intense stress caused blood to seep out of His sweat glands.

After His arrest, Jesus was flogged so mercilessly that His skin was stripped off His back, exposing muscle and bone. The soldiers who tortured Jesus would have used a weapon called a flagellum—a whip that had several leather strands with lead balls or shards of bone attached to the ends. The cuts inflicted by this whip could actually rip open the flesh and expose internal organs. Jesus would have lost a significant amount of blood after His scourging—and this would explain why He did not have the strength to carry His cross all the way to Calvary.

Matthew 27:28–29 says the Roman soldiers stripped Jesus naked and then twisted together a handmade crown of thorns to mock His kingship. Bible scholars believe these thorns were extremely long and hard. When the thorns pierced the top and sides of His head, Jesus would have most likely experienced what doctors call trigeminal neuralgia—piercing pain all over the head and face.[3]

After this horrific abuse, Jesus was covered with a red robe and led to Golgotha. There Roman soldiers drove seven-inch metal spikes into His wrists (most likely hitting the median nerve, causing more blinding pain), and then they rammed another spike into His feet. At that point, doctors say, Jesus would have suffered dislocation of His shoulders, cramps and spasms, dehydration from severe blood loss, fluid in His lungs, and eventual lung collapse and heart failure.

Some victims of Roman crucifixion took as long as nine days to die, but Jesus' death came in a matter of hours—probably because He had been flogged so cruelly before He was nailed to the rough wood. Victims of crucifixion typically developed serious dehydration because of a lack of blood and oxygen.

Jesus willingly poured out His blood on that cruel cross. It was an ugly, revolting, disgusting scene. The Bible does not soften the impact or censor the cruelty of Jesus' suffering. Isaiah 53:6 says: "But the LORD has caused the iniquity of us all to fall on Him."

God laid the sins of the world on Jesus, and then He sacrificed Him as the one and only Lamb of God. Also, Isaiah 53:5 says: "But He was pierced through for our transgressions, He was crushed for our iniquities." He took all that pain to fully pay the price so we could be forgiven.

If you have put your trust in Jesus, asked Him to forgive you, and invited Him to come into your life, you have experienced what the Bible calls salvation. You are free from guilt, the wall of separation between you and God is gone, and you have received the free gift of eternal life. The courts of heaven have declared you not guilty!

LET'S GO **DEEPER**

1. Before Jesus was crucified, He voluntarily took upon Himself the sins of the world. The Father actually laid all the sins of the world on Jesus. Read Mark 14:33–36. What did Jesus say about His decision to "drink the cup" of suffering?

_____

_____

_____

After Jesus made the decision to take the world's sins on Himself, He was arrested, mercilessly whipped, spat upon, mocked, and then crucified by some Roman soldiers. You can read about this in Mark 15:22–37. Keep in mind that the crucifixion of Jesus was an actual event in human history that has been documented. This is not a fable. Soldiers pounded nails into His hands and feet and put a crown of thorns on His head.

Look up these scriptures and write what Jesus' death on the cross actually did for us:

2. Galatians 1:4

_____

3. Romans 5:10

_____

4. 1 Peter 1:18–19

_____

5. Hebrews 9:12

_____

6. When we believe in Jesus and confess our sins to Him, what does He do for us now, according to 1 John 1:9?

_____

_____

_____

LET'S **TALK** ABOUT IT

How does it make you feel when you read about how Jesus suffered for us?

Memory Verse

For God so loved the world that he gave his one and only Son, that whoever believes in him shall not perish but have eternal life. For God did not send his Son into the world to condemn the world, but to save the world through him.

—JOHN 3:16–17, NIV

LET'S GO EVEN DEEPER

Eight Ways Jesus Suffered for Us

We have a detailed written record of the crucifixion of Jesus, but sometimes we read through this hurriedly and overlook how much pain He experienced. Here are eight things we should ponder as we consider His sufferings:

1. He was betrayed by His disciple Judas. Jesus' pain was not just physical. Can you imagine the sorrow He felt when one of His trusted friends became the ultimate traitor? All the pain Jesus endured on Good Friday began the night before, when Judas took blood money to have his Master arrested. We aren't exactly sure how to calculate the modern value of the thirty pieces of silver Judas was paid, but many scholars suggest it was about $950. There's a bit of Judas in all of us, and we all betrayed Jesus to get our way. Yet He chose to forgive us.

2. He was abandoned by His other followers. We often focus on Peter's denial of Jesus. But the Scriptures remind us that all of Jesus' disciples "left Him and fled" after His arrest (Mark 14:50). Jesus had to suffer alone. All the men He had taught and invested in for three and a half years abandoned Him in His hour of need. Jesus accomplished His work of redemption without our help. But He forgave us for our denials.

3. He carried the burden of the sins of the world. Jesus' greatest agony didn't start on the cross. It began at Gethsemane, where God laid on His Son the sins of the world. Jesus agonized so intensely in those moments that He sweat drops of blood (Luke 22:44). Scholars say He probably developed a condition known as hematidrosis, in which blood is emitted through the sweat glands because of intense stress.[4] Your sin was transferred to Jesus' account, and He bore the punishment you deserved.

4. He was falsely accused and rejected by Jewish leaders. Can you imagine the heartache Jesus experienced when the very people He was sent to save spat in His face, blindfolded Him, cursed Him, and accused Him of blasphemy? The Sanhedrin set up a kangaroo court and sentenced the Son of God to death. Jesus did not open His mouth in self-defense when He was falsely accused. Now, when Satan accuses you, Jesus argues your case and declares you not guilty.

5. He was mocked and abused by Roman guards. After Pilate caved in to pressure from the Jews, Roman soldiers flogged Jesus with a whip, drove a crown of thorns into His scalp, beat His head with sticks, and mockingly pretended to worship Him. The flogging alone—which would have involved leather cords with pieces of lead or bone attached—would have drained much of Jesus' blood. Jesus could have called on angels to stop His torture, but He chose to endure the pain because He loved us.

6. He was crucified between two thieves. We cannot even fathom the pain of crucifixion. Metal spikes were driven into Jesus' hands and feet, and He had to slide His mangled body up against the wood of the cross to breathe. And because it was the habit of Romans to crucify criminals naked, Jesus endured the ultimate shame. What's more, He hung on that crude cross next to two men who had been convicted of crimes—while He was completely innocent. We should have been on death row, not Jesus. But He took our place.

7. His body was pierced with a spear. Even after Jesus took His last breath, a soldier jabbed a spear up through the chest cavity—most likely to make sure Jesus was dead. John tells us that blood and water spilled out (John 19:34), evidence that the spear pierced the pericardium, the sac around the heart. Jesus' heart was literally broken for us.

Just as Adam's side was opened to bring forth the first woman, Jesus' side was opened to bring forth the church. His piercing produced a fountain of life for us!

8. He tasted death for all. This is the most horrible reality of the cross. Christ did not die metaphorically or symbolically. He died literally. The Son of God, who had never sinned—and who was least deserving of death—died so we could have life. His heart stopped beating, He stopped breathing, and His spirit left Him. First Peter 3:18 says: "For Christ also died for sins once for all, the just for the unjust, so that He might bring us to God."

Because Jesus died in our place, we no longer have to die. Eternal life is His free gift to us. Don't wait until Resurrection Sunday each year to ponder the steps the Savior took from Gethsemane to Golgotha. Look at His nail-pierced hands and feet. Take a careful survey of His wondrous cross, and thank Him for hanging there six hours for you.

HEROES OF OUR FAITH

MARY OF BETHANY

She Anointed Jesus for His Burial

In the days of Jesus, women were not allowed to receive theological training, and Jewish rabbis did not have female disciples. This is why Mary of Bethany, the sister of Lazarus and Martha, was such a brave pioneer. When Jesus was teaching His male disciples at the home of Lazarus in Luke 10:38-42, Mary defied tradition by sitting at Jesus' feet and listening to His word. She knew that Jesus welcomed her to learn from Him, even though other religious leaders had disdain for women.

Mary was also an eyewitness of Jesus' miracles. In fact, Jesus raised her own brother, Lazarus, from the dead—even though Lazarus had been in the tomb for four days. This must have caused her to realize that Jesus was truly the Son of God. After the miracle, many people who talked to Mary became believers too (John 11:45). She became an evangelist!

Mary also did something very special before Jesus went to the cross. The Bible says that while Jesus was visiting His friends at the home of Lazarus, Mary took some very costly perfume and poured it on His feet in front of all the guests. This was a radical act because only servants would perform such a task, and some people considered it wasteful since the perfume was so expensive.

Why did Mary do this? Jesus Himself said in Matthew 26:12 that Mary was anointing Him for burial. She understood that Jesus was the Son of God and that He was going to die to pay for our sins. Her act of costly devotion was a dramatic form of worship, offered in thanksgiving to Jesus for His sacrifice. Jesus praised Mary for her devotion and said: "Wherever this gospel is preached in the whole world, what this woman has done will also be spoken of in memory of her" (Matthew 26:13). Jesus declared that Mary would be one of the most famous women in the world—because she loved her Savior so much. Mary is now a model of worship for all Christians.

Death Is Defeated

The Power of Christ's Resurrection

"I became a Christian because the evidence was so compelling
that Jesus really is the one-and-only Son of God who proved his
divinity by rising from the dead. That meant following him was
the most rational and logical step I could possibly take."

—LEE STROBEL (1952–)
AUTHOR OF *THE CASE FOR CHRIST*

THERE ARE MANY religions in the world, but Christianity is the only religion whose founder died and was actually raised from the dead. Confucius started Confucianism, but he died in 479 BC. Buddha started Buddhism, but he died somewhere around 483 BC. Muhammad started the Islamic faith, but he died in AD 632.

In the case of Christianity, Jesus Christ actually predicted that He would be crucified, killed, buried, and then raised to life. That is exactly what happened. And this miracle didn't occur in secret. It is a matter of historic record, and more than five hundred people witnessed it.

Imagine that a murder happened in broad daylight on a busy street corner of your city, and more than five hundred people witnessed it. Some of them may have even taken cell phone videos or photos of the crime. All these witnesses appeared in a courtroom, stood on the witness stand, swore in front of a judge that they would tell the truth, and then testified that they knew who the murderer was. Any jury would find that criminal guilty because of the overwhelming evidence. That is why the resurrection of Jesus is considered fact—even though it is an astounding miracle that defies the normal rules of science.

When the Gospel writer Luke wrote about the witnesses of Jesus' resurrection, he said, "To these He also presented Himself alive after His suffering, *by many convincing proofs*, appearing to them over a period of forty days and speaking of the things concerning the kingdom of God"

(Acts 1:3, emphasis added). Luke had no doubt that Jesus had been raised from the dead because there was so much evidence.

The apostle Paul also spoke of these witnesses. He wrote in 1 Corinthians 15:3–8:

> For I delivered to you as of first importance what I also received, that Christ died for our sins according to the Scriptures, and that He was buried, and that He was raised on the third day according to the Scriptures, and that He appeared to Cephas, then to the twelve. After that He appeared to more than five hundred brethren at one time, most of whom remain until now, but some have fallen asleep; then He appeared to James, then to all the apostles; and last of all, as to one untimely born, He appeared to me also.

Of course, for centuries doubters and skeptics have tried to disprove the resurrection by concocting various conspiracy theories. They have claimed, for example, that Jesus' followers went to the wrong tomb to find His body; that the early disciples experienced a "group hallucination"; that Jesus had not really died but was rather just unconscious after the brutal abuse His body experienced (this is known as "the swoon theory"); or that Jesus' body was stolen and never found. None of these theories are plausible.[1]

Consider, for example, that in two thousand years no one ever produced the "stolen body" of Jesus! As for the swoon theory, it is laughable to think that Jesus could have survived after a soldier thrust a spear into His side and pierced His heart. That kind of medical recovery would be impossible today, even with modern medical technology.

Journalist Lee Strobel, who actually tried to disprove the claims of Christianity by researching ancient documents and interviewing scholars, became a Christian evangelist after he came face to face with the overwhelming evidence of the resurrection. He wrote many books, including his most popular, *The Case for Christ*. Strobel said of the hallucination theory: "I went to a psychologist friend and said if 500 people claimed to see Jesus after he died, it was just a hallucination. He said hallucinations are an individual event. If 500 people have the same hallucination, that's a bigger miracle than the resurrection."[2]

For centuries intelligent scholars and even criminal lawyers who have studied the evidence have gone on record to say that the resurrection of Jesus is a fact.

Sir Edward Clark, who served as a solicitor general in the Victorian era in England, wrote: "As a lawyer, I have made a prolonged study of the evidences for the events of the first Easter day. To me the evidence is conclusive, and over and over again in the High Court I have secured the verdict on evidence not nearly so compelling. Inference follows on evidence, and a truthful witness is always artless and disdains effect. The gospel evidence for the resurrection is of this class, and as a lawyer I accept it unreservedly as a testimony of truthful men to facts they were able to substantiate."[3]

There are mountains of evidence for us to ponder when we consider the resurrection. The huge stone on Jesus' tomb was miraculously moved (it probably weighed between one and two tons); the Roman seal on the grave was broken; Jesus' graveclothes were left behind; and the Roman guards disappeared.

In addition, more than five hundred people saw Jesus and heard Him talk after He resurrected. Some of them, like the apostle Thomas, actually touched His nail scars. The apostle John wrote that not only did he see the risen Christ, but he also touched Him (1 John 1:1).

But perhaps the greatest evidence of Jesus' resurrection is not that hundreds of people in the first century saw Him but that they were willing to be jailed, stoned, thrown into arenas with savage animals, or burned alive because they would not renounce their belief in Jesus Christ. Almost all the early disciples became martyrs.

Roman citizens were required to pledge their full allegiance to Rome and declare that Caesar was a god—but early Christians were willing to go to their deaths because they knew the risen Christ was the true Lord of all. Their courage should inspire us to be brave witnesses of the resurrection of Jesus in our lifetime.

One well-known American pastor, Adrian Rogers, said this: "The resurrection is not merely important to the historic Christian faith; without it, there would be no Christianity. It is the singular doctrine that elevates Christianity above all other world religions."[4] Never doubt that Jesus walked out of that tomb alive. This is the foundation of all we believe.

LET'S GO **DEEPER**

1. In Matthew 16:21–23, Jesus tells His disciples He is going to be killed by His enemies. In verse 22 how does Peter react to this information?

_____

_____

2. In Matthew 20:18–19, Jesus told His disciples clearly what would happen to Him at the end of His ministry. What did He warn them about?

_____

_____

After Jesus died, His body was put in a stone tomb, a giant stone was rolled in front of the entrance, and Roman guards kept watch to make sure no one tried to remove it. But on the third day, when some of Jesus' female disciples came to the tomb to bring embalming spices, an angel came from heaven and rolled the stone away.

3. The Roman guards were traumatized, but the angel gave the women an important message. What did the angel say in Matthew 28:5–7?

_____

_____

_____

4. Read John 20:26–29. After the resurrection Jesus appeared to His disciples and gave them a chance to see and touch His wounded hands and His pierced side. What did Jesus tell Thomas after Thomas touched Jesus and called Him "my Lord and my God"?

_____

_____

_____

5. Jesus stayed on earth forty days after His resurrection, appearing to His witnesses and giving evidence of His authority. According to 1 Corinthians 15:3–8, to whom did Jesus appear?

_____

_____

_____

6. Read 1 Corinthians 15:12–17. During the first century there were some false teachers who denied that Jesus had risen from the dead. Why is the doctrine of the resurrection so important to us as believers in Christ?

_____

_____

_____

LET'S **TALK** ABOUT IT

How would you respond to a person who says the resurrection is a hoax?

Memory Verse

If you confess with your mouth Jesus as Lord, and believe in your heart that God raised Him from the dead, you will be saved.

—Romans 10:9

HEROES OF OUR FAITH

PETER

Jesus Called Him a Rock

When Jesus called a humble fisherman named Simon to follow Him as a disciple, He gave him a new name. Jesus said, "You are Simon the son of John; you shall be called Cephas (which is translated Peter)" (John 1:42). Cephas means "rock."[1] Peter did not always act like a sturdy rock, but Jesus saw amazing potential in this man. He also declared that Peter would become a fisher of men (Mark 1:17).

Peter certainly showed leadership skills as Jesus trained him. But Peter was also a bit unstable. On some days he was passionately following Jesus; on other days he put his foot in his mouth, and Jesus had to rebuke him. Peter was the first disciple to declare that Jesus was the Son of God, yet when Jesus said He would sacrifice His life, Peter said, "God forbid it, Lord! This shall never happen to You" (Matthew 16:22). Peter was always unpredictable.

On the night before Jesus' execution, Peter denied that he even knew Jesus—three times!—and then he became deeply depressed. Peter felt like a failure. Yet after Jesus rose from the dead, He found Peter by the seashore and asked him again to follow Him. Jesus did not disqualify Peter because of his mistakes. Instead He restored him—and Peter became a strong leader among the apostles who took the gospel all over Israel. In fact, when Peter preached the gospel on the day of Pentecost, three thousand people repented and began following Christ (Acts 2:41). Peter's story reminds us that Jesus can turn His unstable followers into strong, steadfast "rocks" who will make a huge impact on the world.

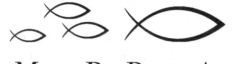

You Must Be Born Again

The Miracle of Spiritual Conversion

"Amazing grace! How sweet the sound, that saved a wretch like me!
I once was lost, but now am found, was blind, but now I see."
—JOHN NEWTON (1725–1807)
BRITISH SLAVE TRADER WHO BECAME AN ABOLITIONIST AFTER HIS CONVERSION

LONG AGO AN Old Testament prophet named Ezekiel saw a vision of a valley full of dry bones. Then God asked the prophet, "Can these bones live?" That surely did not look possible, but God told Ezekiel to prophesy to the dry bones. Suddenly the bones stood, then flesh appeared on them, and then skin. Then the bodies began breathing!

This vision shows us what happens when a sinful person puts their faith in Jesus Christ and asks for God's forgiveness. Ephesians 2:5 says, "Even when we were dead in our transgressions," God "made us alive together with Christ." This is the miracle we call the new birth. When your sin separated you from God, you were like a dead body, or a dry skeleton. But when you experience the miracle of salvation, you receive the gift of supernatural life from God. The power of sin is broken, your spirit becomes alive, and you are able to have a relationship with your Creator.

When Jesus began His ministry on earth, a Jewish man named Nicodemus came to Him to find out if He was the true Son of God. Nicodemus was a very moral and religious man, and he assumed that he would be first in line to have eternal life with God. But Jesus said something very curious to Nicodemus. He said: "Truly, truly, I say to you, unless one is born again he cannot see the kingdom of God" (John 3:3). Nicodemus realized that all his good works and religious efforts could not save him. He needed an inner transformation.

Jesus told Nicodemus that all human beings must be "born again" to see heaven and the person who believes He is the Son of God receives the gift of eternal life. A miracle takes place in the human heart when we believe. When you put your faith in Jesus, an invisible transformation occurs. The Holy Spirit enters your heart and makes His permanent residence there. You receive the gift of eternal life, which means you will go to heaven when you die. But most importantly you begin a lifelong journey of knowing Christ in a personal way.

When the Holy Spirit enters your life, the Bible says you are "adopted" by God as His own beloved child. Romans 8:15 says: "You have received a spirit of adoption as sons by which we cry out, 'Abba! Father!'" The word *abba* is the Hebrew word for *daddy*. When you experience salvation you suddenly feel connected to your merciful heavenly Father. He forgives your sins, makes you a new creation, and begins a friendship with you.

Jesus told Nicodemus that we are born again by the Holy Spirit (John 3:5). True conversion is the most supernatural thing we will ever experience. When a person puts his faith in Christ for salvation, it is the Spirit who opens the heart and imparts divine life. He then indwells us—and He gives us the confidence that we are now children of God. None of us would be Christians today if it were not for the regenerating power of the Spirit. If you are praying for someone to repent and give his or her heart to Jesus, do not minimize the role the Holy Spirit plays in this process.

We typically tell new Christians that Jesus came into their hearts at the moment they repented of their sins. But again, our language limits the grandeur of a true conversion. When the Holy Spirit enters the life of a repentant believer, He literally breathes new life into the dead! Just as the prophet Ezekiel watched dry bones stand up, grow new flesh, and breathe again (Ezekiel 37), people who are dead in sin are resurrected to a new life when they believe in Jesus Christ.

Of all the manifestations of the Holy Spirit available to us, conversion is the most precious—and the most astounding. Never minimize the Holy Spirit's power to transform a sinner.

LET'S GO **DEEPER**

1. According to Ephesians 2:1, what condition were you in before you met Christ?

_____

2. Read Romans 10:9. What must a person do to be saved from sin?

_____

_____

3. According to 1 Peter 1:23, what causes us to be born again?

_____

4. Read Acts 4:12. What do we need to do to be saved from our sins, according to this verse?

_____

5. Read 2 Corinthians 5:17. What happens to a person after they experience true conversion?

_____

6. According to John 17:3, what is the definition of *eternal life*?

_____

LET'S **TALK** ABOUT IT

Share the story of your own conversion. How did Jesus change your life after you decided to follow Him?

Memory Verse

Therefore if anyone is in Christ, he is a new creature; the old things passed away; behold, new things have come.

—2 CORINTHIANS 5:17

HEROES OF OUR FAITH

MARK

The Apostle Peter's Spiritual Son

Also known as John Mark in the Bible, this man may have been a teenager during the time Jesus was preaching in Israel. He lived in Jerusalem, and his family must have been early followers of Christ. He was related to Barnabas, a respected leader of the early church, and Mark traveled with Barnabas and the apostle Paul on their first apostolic journey.

During that trip to Asia Minor, Mark abandoned the team. (See Acts 15:38.) The Bible doesn't tell us why Mark gave up—he may have been homesick, or perhaps the fear of persecution was too much for him. All we know is that Paul didn't want Mark to work with him anymore because of his unfaithfulness. Barnabas, on the other hand, felt more merciful toward Mark, who was his cousin, and this disagreement separated Paul and Barnabas.

In the end we know that Paul reconciled with Mark, and they traveled together again and were on good terms. We also know that Mark ended up being very close to the apostle Peter, who refers to Mark as "my son" in his first epistle (1 Peter 5:13). Mark eventually wrote one of the four Gospels based on Peter's eyewitness testimony. His life shows us that we should never give up on people because of their failures. Mark was a bit untrustworthy when he was a young man, but he became strong in faith, and his recorded history of Jesus' ministry is an inspired record of the miracles of Jesus.

Buried With Christ

Why We Need Water Baptism

"I thought I could have leaped from earth to heaven at one spring
when I first saw my sins drowned in the Redeemer's blood."
—CHARLES H. SPURGEON (1834–1892)
BRITISH PREACHER AND AUTHOR

BEFORE JESUS ASCENDED into heaven He told His disciples to baptize people in water after they made the decision to believe in Him. Jesus said in Matthew 28:19: "Go therefore and make disciples of all the nations, baptizing them in the name of the Father and the Son and the Holy Spirit."

The Christians of the early New Testament weren't the first people to practice baptism. Jews practiced this ritual of immersing a person in water as a way to symbolize purification from sins. In fact, Jesus' cousin, John, earned his famous title "John the Baptist" because he challenged people to repent of their sins and then undergo baptism in water to seal their decision. Many Jews were baptized by John the Baptist just prior to the time Jesus began His ministry.

Jesus Himself was baptized by John in the Jordan River, not because Jesus needed cleansing from sin but because He was setting an example for us all. As a forerunner of faith, Jesus paved the way for us to experience a new life with God. Even though He didn't need to repent—because He had no sin—He went into the waters first for us so that we could receive His amazing grace.

After Jesus paid for our sins on the cross, His followers immediately began practicing baptism. On the day of Pentecost, when three thousand people were converted after hearing Peter's sermon, the crowd asked Peter what they should do to be saved. Peter told them:

> Repent, and each of you be baptized in the name of Jesus Christ
> for the forgiveness of your sins; and you will receive the gift of
> the Holy Spirit.
>
> —ACTS 2:38

As we read the history of the early church in the Book of Acts, we learn that new Christians were baptized after Philip's evangelistic campaign in Samaria (Acts 8:12–13); the Ethiopian convert was baptized in the desert (Acts 8:36–40); Saul was baptized after his dramatic conversion (Acts 9:18); some Italian converts were baptized in Caesarea (Acts 10:47–48); Lydia was baptized in Philippi (Acts 16:15); and the Philippian jailer and his family were baptized after he decided to follow Christ (Acts 16:33). In the early church baptism in water was always the first step for a new Christian.

This practice has continued throughout the two thousand years of Christianity, until today. It doesn't matter where people are baptized— it can happen in a lake, a river, an ocean, a swimming pool, a Jacuzzi, a bathtub, or even a horse trough. I have seen a video of a baptism in Russia where a pastor cut a hole in ice and eager believers were plunged into a frigid Siberian lake! People are baptized out of obedience to Christ, but also to mark the fact that a decision to follow Jesus is a *defining moment* in anyone's life.

This practice may seem a bit odd to us today. Why would Jesus want His followers to go to the trouble of being submerged in water after they repent of their sins and believe in Him? It will help if we recall an ancient event from the Old Testament to understand the full significance of water baptism.

In the Book of Exodus we read the fascinating story of how God delivered the Hebrew people out of their captivity in Egypt. They had been slaves there for 430 years, and the pharaoh didn't want to let them go. He needed them for free labor to build his temples and pyramids. Yet God anointed Moses with His authority to demand that the pharaoh release the slaves so they could go to the land that God had given them.

God poured out His fierce judgment on Egypt by sending ten terrible plagues, but the hard-hearted pharaoh stubbornly refused to budge. Finally, after the final plague killed every firstborn male child in the land, the wicked ruler permitted the Hebrews to pack up their belongings hurriedly and leave. Then, just when the Israelites reached the shore of the Red Sea on their journey to Canaan, Pharaoh sent his army to capture them again.

As the Egyptian warriors approached in their chariots, Moses told the people of Israel: "The LORD will fight for you while you keep silent" (Exodus 14:14). Then God said to Moses: "As for you, lift up your staff and stretch out your hand over the sea and divide it, and the sons of Israel shall go through the midst of the sea on dry land" (v. 16).

And that is exactly what happened: Moses stretched out his arm over the sea, and God parted the waters so that the Hebrews were able to walk through the seabed on dry land. When they reached the other side of the sea, the waters returned to their normal level, drowning Pharaoh's army. The enemy's chariots, horses, and weapons all sank into the murky waters. God had supernaturally defeated the powerful pharaoh.

Then Moses sang a song to the Lord that said:

> I will sing to the LORD, for He is highly exalted; the horse and its rider He has hurled into the sea. The LORD is my strength and song, and He has become my salvation.
>
> —EXODUS 15:1-2

The Jewish people celebrated this remarkable story of Israel's deliverance for hundreds of years after the Red Sea parted. The miracle happened thirty-five hundred years ago, but it became the most talked-about event of the Old Testament. It is what we call a *defining moment* for Israel.

It also has powerful symbolic meaning for Christians today. Israel passing through the Red Sea is a foreshadowing of Christians being submerged in the waters of baptism. Just as God destroyed death and slavery in the waters of the Red Sea, liberating His people to serve Him in their new land, so was death and the bondage of sin destroyed when Jesus Christ redeemed us on the cross.

When we believe in Him, and we are baptized in water, we are reminded that we are free from sin and the devil's power. Satan wanted us to be slaves of sin, but God defeated him by sending Jesus. Just as Moses parted the waters of the Red Sea, Jesus made a way for us to have eternal life. This is what we celebrate every time someone is baptized. It is a powerful way of publicly declaring what Jesus has done for us:

- Baptism is a powerful reminder that Jesus has washed us clean.

- Baptism symbolizes the death and resurrection of Jesus. When we go into the water, we are reminded that Christ died for us; when we come out of the water, we declare that Jesus has been raised from the dead.

- Baptism is a powerful pronouncement that we have shut the door forever to our past sins. When we are baptized, we renounce Satan, his demons, and all false idols. We pledge our full allegiance to Jesus by being baptized in His name.

- Baptism gives a new believer the opportunity to identify as a Christian in front of others. Jesus said, "Therefore everyone who confesses Me before men, I will also confess him before My Father who is in heaven" (Matthew 10:32).

If you have chosen to follow Jesus as your Lord, you should plan to take the important step of public baptism in water if you have not already done so. This step of obedience will be a defining moment in your walk with Christ.

LET'S GO **DEEPER**

1. Read Romans 6:3–7. According to this passage, what does water baptism do for us?

_____

_____

_____

2. Read Colossians 2:12–13. Describe what happens to a Christian during water baptism.

_____

_____

_____

3. What is another thing that happens to us when we are baptized, according to Galatians 3:27?

_____

4. Read Acts 22:15–16. When Paul was converted to Jesus, Ananias told him to quickly get baptized. Why do you think it is important to be baptized without delay?

_____

_____

_____

LET'S **TALK** ABOUT IT

Have you already been baptized in water? If not, what is preventing you from doing it?

Memory Verse

Therefore we have been buried with Him through baptism into death, so that as Christ was raised from the dead through the glory of the Father, so we too might walk in newness of life.

—ROMANS 6:4

HEROES OF OUR FAITH

MATTHEW

He Understood the Messiah's Mission

Matthew was raised as a Jew in Israel, but he was an unlikely candidate to follow a Jewish rabbi like Jesus. That's because Matthew was a tax collector; he would have been considered a traitor by his fellow countrymen because he was fraternizing with Roman soldiers and supporting their economic oppression. When Matthew decided to follow Jesus, he hosted a party at his house. The judgmental Pharisees criticized Jesus when they saw Him with Matthew and his friends, and they asked why Jesus was "eating with the tax collectors and sinners" (Matthew 9:11). Perhaps Jesus looked directly at His new disciple, Matthew, when He answered: "I did not come to call the righteous, but sinners" (v. 13).

Despite Matthew's sinful background, Jesus chose him to be an important witness of His life and ministry. Matthew had a special goal to prove to Jewish people that Jesus was the Messiah promised by Old Testament writers such as Micah, Hosea, Jeremiah, Isaiah, Malachi, David, and Moses. Matthew quotes those men twenty-nine times, more than any other Gospel writer. He ingeniously structured his Gospel in a unique way around five sermons of Jesus. This would have reminded Jews of the Torah, the first five books of the Old Testament, which were written by Moses. Some scholars have called the Gospel of Matthew "a new Torah."[1]

Matthew subtly compares Jesus to Moses in his Gospel, but he dramatically proves that Jesus was better than Moses in every way. In the Old Testament, Moses went on top of Mount Sinai and received the Ten Commandments from God. In Matthew's Gospel, Jesus went on top of a mountain and preached about the attitudes of love, humility, patience, gentleness, and purity we should have in our hearts. Moses gave us a list of rules to perform, but Jesus gives us grace so the Law can be written in our hearts. Matthew pointed all Jews—and the rest of the world—to the Messiah, who came from heaven to save us.

The Greatest Book of All

Why Christians Cherish the Bible

"I believe the Bible is the best gift God has ever given to man. All the good from the Savior of the world is communicated to us through this Book."

—ABRAHAM LINCOLN (1809–1865)
SIXTEENTH PRESIDENT OF THE UNITED STATES

ONE OF THE first things you will notice when you become a Christian is that all of your new Christian friends love the Bible. They read it regularly, they gather in small groups to study it, they listen to pastors preach about it, they sing about it, and they watch online videos about it. Many Christians also memorize Bible verses or hang their favorite scriptures on the walls of their homes. The Bible is obviously very important to people who are following Jesus. But why?

The Bible is a very unusual book. More than forty different authors wrote parts of the Bible over a span of sixteen hundred years, yet the core message seems dramatically consistent. The sixty-six books of the Bible were written by prophets, kings, historians, priests, shepherds, soldiers, fishermen, and even a physician. The original texts were written on ancient papyrus and then faithfully copied and recopied. Yet somehow this exceptional book has been preserved intact for us today.

From beginning to end, from Genesis to Revelation, the message of the Bible focuses on a loving God who has a plan to redeem the human race from sin so they can know and worship Him forever. The Old Testament was written in the Hebrew language, and the New Testament was written in Greek, yet today the entire Bible has been translated into more than 717 languages.[2] It is the best-selling book of all time. Although Bible publishing is difficult to track globally, one recent study showed that between 5 and 7 billion Bibles have been sold.[3] The Bible seems to have universal appeal to readers all over the world.

Christians have three core beliefs about God's Word.

1. The Bible was supernaturally inspired by God. The words of the Bible are not simply human wisdom or philosophy; Christians believe the Holy Spirit divinely spoke to the authors of the Bible and gave them the words. This is confirmed in 2 Peter 1:20–21:

> But know this first of all, that no prophecy of Scripture is a matter of one's own interpretation, for no prophecy was ever made by an act of human will, but men moved by the Holy Spirit spoke from God.

This should encourage you to treat the Bible with awe and respect. This is no ordinary book! It is a love letter sent from God's heart to yours. This is why we call the Bible "the Word of God."

2. The Bible was supernaturally compiled and preserved by God. If God inspired different writers to write down His message to the world, then God certainly had the power to protect those words and put them in a book for us to read. Christians believe God worked through His followers over the centuries to compile these sacred writings and to prevent any uninspired writings from being included.

In the Old Testament period faithful Jews preserved the ancient scrolls of Moses, David, Isaiah, Solomon, Jeremiah, and other writers, and they shared a consensus about what books were divinely inspired. These thirty-nine books became the "canon," or "standard," of the collected Old Testament Scriptures. The same thing occurred in the early New Testament period, when leaders of the church were led by the Holy Spirit to publish and recommend only the writings that carried divine inspiration. That's why the New Testament has its twenty-seven books.

And so we have the Bible in its present form. Early church leaders also taught that the Bible concluded with the Revelation of the apostle John and that no other books of the Bible were needed. They considered the canon of Scripture closed. John's amen in the last verse of the Bible, Revelation 22:21, marks the end of the Bible.

3. The Bible is supernaturally sufficient for us. Jesus taught that we should love the Scriptures more than our daily food. When He was tempted in the wilderness, He told the devil:

It is written, "Man shall not live on bread alone, but on every word that proceeds out of the mouth of God."

—MATTHEW 4:4

In other words, the Bible contains everything we need. It provides wisdom for daily life, counsel for our problems, comfort for our grief, warnings about our sinful nature, and theological insight into the ways and character of God.

The Bible is our ultimate source for truth. We don't have to look to any other spiritual source to find truth about God. We won't find it in the Quran, in Hindu texts, in Buddhist writings, or in books about New Age or the occult. We don't have to look for the meaning of life in the writings of worldly philosophers. If we try to find truth in other religions, we will end up dissatisfied and deceived. The Bible has in it what we need. It is our daily bread.

LET'S GO **DEEPER**

Psalm 119 is almost at the very center of the Bible, and it is the longest chapter in the Bible. Interestingly, the entire psalm is about the importance of the Scriptures. This is why I call it the "spine" of the Bible. At the very core of the Bible is an important psalm that calls us to cherish God's Word.

Read these verses in Psalm 119 and list the benefits of reading God's Word.

1. Psalm 119:5–6

_____

2. Psalm 119:9–10

_____

3. Psalm 119:11

_____

4. Psalm 119:104

_____

5. Psalm 119:105

_____

6. Psalm 119:129–130

_____

7. Psalm 119:133

_____

8. If we truly believe the Bible is God's inspired Word, coming directly from Him, we just submit to its authority in our lives. Read Hebrews 4:12 and write down the effect God's Word will have on us.

_____

_____

_____

9. Read 2 Timothy 3:16–17. In what ways will Scripture help us if we accept it as God's inspired Word?

_____

_____

_____

10. Read Luke 11:28. It is not enough just to read the Bible. What else must we do?

_____

_____

LET'S **TALK** ABOUT IT

What could you do to give God's Word a higher priority in your life than you do currently?

Memory Verse

The sum of Your word is truth, and every one of Your righteous ordinances is everlasting.

—PSALM 119:160

HEROES OF OUR FAITH

JOHN THE BAPTIST

He Prepared the Way for the Lord

The son of a Jewish priest, John the Baptist was the last of the great Old Testament prophets. Before his birth an angel declared that he would be like the mighty Elijah and that he would turn the people's hearts back to God. It was also prophesied that John would "make ready a people prepared for the Lord" (Luke 1:17). His unique job was to clear a path for Jesus Christ to come into this world.

And that's what happened. Jesus was born just six months after John. At a chaotic time in Israel's history when Roman soldiers oppressed the Jewish people, John began preaching a forceful message of repentance. He was like a spiritual bulldozer, demanding repentance from pride, greed, hatred, and selfishness as he carried on his ministry in the wilderness near the river Jordan. John called the Jews back to their first love, and he baptized hundreds of people.

But when Jesus showed up at the river's edge to be baptized—and to begin His mission of redemption—John looked at Him and declared, "Behold, the Lamb of God who takes away the sin of the world!" (John 1:29). Because of the special anointing on John (he had been filled with the Holy Spirit since he was in his mother's womb), he understood Jesus' purpose like few others. He also said of Jesus, "After me comes a Man who has a higher rank than I, for He existed before me" (John 1:30). John knew that Jesus was the Son of God, who had come from heaven to rescue humanity—and to usher in a new covenant of grace and forgiveness.

It took great humility for this fiery preacher to stand to the side and allow Jesus to take center stage. John knew he had to decrease and that Jesus would increase. Rather than calling people to himself, John pointed the Jews to Jesus and urged them to follow Him. He was a faithful witness of Jesus even up to the moment when he was beheaded by King Herod. He reminds us even today that we all must prepare our hearts to receive the Lord.

The Law in Our Hearts

Why God Made a New Covenant

"In the Old Covenant man had failed in what he had to do. In the New, God is to do everything in him. The Old could only convict of sin. The New is to put it away and cleanse the heart from its filthiness. In the Old it was the heart that was wrong; for the New a new heart is provided."

—ANDREW MURRAY (1828–1917)
SOUTH AFRICAN PASTOR AND WRITER

WHEN WE LIST a date in history we often mention whether the year is "BC," which means "Before Christ," or "AD," which is the abbreviation for *anno Domini*, the Latin phrase for "in the year of our Lord."[1] This means that the coming of Jesus Christ into this world actually split time into two parts—the time period before Jesus and the centuries after. That is how important Jesus Christ is in our world!

When we look at the Bible, it also follows this general rule. It is divided into two parts. The Old Testament, also known as the Old Covenant, covers the centuries from creation to the coming of Jesus. The New Testament, or New Covenant, covers the ministry of Jesus and the activity of the Holy Spirit after the death and resurrection of Jesus.

These two covenants are not simply different time periods. They represent two vastly different ways that God interacted with His people. In the days of Moses, God instituted the old covenant system, which we call the Law. In this time period, God gave an elaborate system of rules, regulations, and rituals to His Israelite followers—and He required people to obey His commands or suffer the consequences of sin.

But the Bible says that when Jesus came to this earth and died on the cross for us, His act of redemption inaugurated a new covenant. The old covenant order ended and a new order began. Jesus changed everything! As a Christian you must understand that you now live in the new covenant period, and you can experience the blessings of it.

I hope you realize how blessed you are that you don't live under the restrictions of the old covenant. Here is a partial description of what life was like under the Law:

- After God gave His moral laws, He said that those who obeyed them would be blessed, but those who disobeyed them would be cursed. (See Deuteronomy 28:1–15.) The problem is that all human beings are sinners, so no one can possibly keep all God's laws—not even people who try hard to be morally superior.

  The Law contained many regulations. It required, for instance, that all worshippers attend certain annual festivals, adhere to a strict diet, cease from all labor on the Sabbath, and follow pages and pages of other rules. In reality, a person could never truly please God unless he or she was perfect.

- Because of sin God required His followers to bring animal sacrifices to their place of worship. Depending on their sin they would bring sheep, goats, birds, or grain offerings. The Jewish priests would then slaughter the animals while the worshipper watched; then the worshippers could be ritually cleansed. These sacrifices had to be made regularly.

- Those who worshipped the true God could not draw near to Him, even when they offered animal sacrifices. The average worshipper brought his offerings to the gate of the tabernacle or the temple, and then designated priests would go inside and worship God on behalf of the people.

- Not even the priests could go into the inner sanctuary, where God's presence was. A thick curtain separated the priests from the ark of the covenant, which contained the scrolls of the Law. No one was good enough to appear before God.

- Also, under the old covenant, God was totally focused on the tiny nation of Israel. He called this special people to follow Him, and those who were outside of Israel—the Gentiles—did not benefit in any way from God's blessings. The old covenant was strict, and it was severely limited!

Thankfully, God enacted a new covenant with His people. He used the old covenant to prove to us that human beings cannot achieve holiness on our own. We are hopelessly flawed and sinful. God's rules were perfect and holy, but they had no power to help us become holy—they only revealed our dark nature. So instead of holding an impossible standard of perfection over us, God set aside the old covenant and made a new one. He predicted this through the prophet Jeremiah when He said:

> "Behold, days are coming," declares the LORD, "when I will make a new covenant with the house of Israel and with the house of Judah, not like the covenant which I made with their fathers in the day I took them by the hand to bring them out of the land of Egypt, My covenant which they broke, although I was a husband to them," declares the LORD. "But this is the covenant which I will make with the house of Israel after those days," declares the LORD, "I will put My law within them and on their heart I will write it; and I will be their God, and they shall be My people."
>
> —JEREMIAH 31:31–33

God created a whole new order under this new covenant, and the Book of Hebrews tells us that this new system is "better" in every way. Here's how it works now:

- Instead of requiring endless sacrifices of animals to cleanse us from sin, God sacrificed His own Son, Jesus, who was the perfect sacrifice.

- God puts His Holy Spirit inside every person who believes in Jesus, and the Holy Spirit gives us the power to overcome sin and obey the Lord. This is how God "writes" His law in our hearts, according to Jeremiah 31:33.

- Under the new covenant, we don't have to stand far away from God and worship from a distance. The Bible says when Jesus died on the cross, "the veil of the temple was torn in two from top to bottom" (Matthew 27:51). That symbolized that God was serious about having a close and intimate relationship with His people. With the tearing of that veil, God ended the old covenant system.

- After Jesus paid for our sins, the temple was destroyed and the system of sacrifices ended. God's moral law still stands, but Christians recognize that it is only through the power of the indwelling Christ that we can please God.

- Also, after Jesus paid for our sins, not only Jews but people from every race and nationality could enjoy fellowship with God.

Sometimes writers of the Bible used the words *law* and *grace* to describe the difference between the old and new covenants. For example, John says in his Gospel, "For the Law was given through Moses; grace and truth were realized through Jesus Christ" (John 1:17).

The word *grace* is defined as generous and undeserved favor, and it describes the unmerited love we receive from God because of the merciful sacrifice of Jesus. The laws of Moses required perfect obedience on our part, yet under grace even the worst sinners can find forgiveness.

The word *grace* appears in the Old Testament only nine times—but it appears in the New Testament 122 times. (This is in the 1995 edition of the New American Standard Bible.) Because of the goodness and mercy of Jesus, God's grace is abundant toward us. It should saturate our lives. I hope you are grateful that you live in the age of grace!

LET'S GO **DEEPER**

1. Read Jeremiah 31:31–33. How would you describe the difference between the old covenant and the new covenant?

_____

_____

2. Read Ephesians 2:8–9. This passage says we cannot be saved by keeping the laws of God or by our own performance. How are we saved?

_____

3. Read Romans 8:3. The Law, under the old covenant, was too weak to give us salvation from sin. What did Jesus then do for us?

_____

4. Read Hebrews 4:16. Under the new covenant we do not have to keep a distance from God because He has removed the separation. How should we now approach God?

_____

5. Read 1 John 2:1. Jesus is described in this verse as our "Advocate," which means He is like a lawyer in a courtroom who argues our case and finds us not guilty. If you sin after you begin your walk with Jesus, what should you do?

_____

LET'S **TALK** ABOUT IT

Try to explain the difference between the old and new covenants and why the new covenant is so much better.

Memory Verse

For by grace you have been saved through faith; and that not of yourselves, it is the gift of God; not as a result of works, so that no one may boast.

—EPHESIANS 2:8–9

HEROES OF OUR FAITH

MARY MAGDALENE

A Witness of Christ's Resurrection

Mary Magdalene was one of Jesus' most devoted followers. She must have had a troubled past, because the Bible tells us in Luke 8:2 that Jesus cast seven demons out of her. Yet she was part of Jesus' close circle of friends, and she, along with other women disciples, contributed financially to support Jesus' mission. When Jesus was crucified, Mary bravely stood near the cross and watched Him die.

On the morning that Jesus was raised from the dead, Mary came to the tomb with the other women to tend to His body with embalming spices. There she earned a front-row seat to watch the greatest miracle in history. When she saw that the stone had been rolled away from the sepulcher, she looked inside and saw two angels, one at the head and one at the foot of the grave. When she turned around, the resurrected Jesus was standing there, and He called her name: "Mary!"

His loyal disciple was so shocked to see Jesus alive that she grabbed Him. She could see Him with her eyes, but she wanted to feel with her hands that it really was her Master. Jesus then said to her, "Stop clinging to Me, for I have not yet ascended to the Father; but go to My brethren and say to them, 'I ascend to My Father and your Father, and My God and your God'" (John 20:17). Not only was Mary one of the key witnesses of the resurrection, but Jesus commissioned her to tell His male followers that He had overcome death.

In the days of Jesus, women were not even trusted to be witnesses in a court of law, yet Jesus broke that tradition by calling a woman to announce this glorious news. Mary reminds us today that Jesus still calls broken, unqualified, and marginalized people to spread the good news of His love to the world.

The Enemy of Our Souls

Who Exactly Is the Devil?

"The cleverest ruse of the Devil is to persuade you he does not exist!"
—CHARLES BAUDELAIRE (1821–1867)
FRENCH POET

A S SOON AS Jesus began His ministry in Israel, He had a dramatic encounter with Satan himself. While Jesus was fasting and praying for forty days in the wilderness, the devil came to oppose Him. Just as Satan had tempted Adam and Eve in the Garden of Eden to turn away from God, Satan invited Jesus to fall down and worship him. But unlike Adam and Eve, Jesus was not deceived by the serpent. Jesus quoted Scripture to Satan all three times He was tempted, and Satan eventually left Him. (See Matthew 4:1–11.)

That was not Jesus' last encounter with Satan or his demons. Right after Jesus called Peter, Andrew, James, and John to be His disciples, they went to a synagogue in Capernaum, and a demon-possessed man began to cry out loudly. Jesus rebuked the spirit, and the man went into convulsions until the demon came out. (See Mark 1:21–26.) This scene was repeated often. Jesus cast out so many demons from people, in fact, that the common people were amazed and said, "What is this? A new teaching with authority! He commands even the unclean spirits, and they obey Him" (Mark 1:27).

The Bible teaches us that Satan is a personal, spiritual being who is the ultimate enemy of God. He is not a fictional character. Satan is real, and he has a whole host of followers known as demons, or evil spirits, who serve in a sinister hierarchy to fight against God's plans. You do not have to be afraid of the devil, but as a believer in Christ you must know your enemy. Here are some truths you must know:

The devil is a fallen angel. Satan was originally created as an angel to serve God, but he was cast out of heaven because of his pride. (See

Ezekiel 28.) Hollywood has perpetrated the idea that Satan has horns, a red cape, and a pitchfork, but this idea is based on medieval folklore, not the Bible. In fact, the Bible says the devil is a master of clever disguises and that he prefers to appear as "an angel of light" (2 Corinthians 11:14). Without spiritual discernment, most people don't even recognize that the devil is working.

Satan has a kingdom. Because of man's sin, Satan gained access to manipulate and control this world temporarily. First John 5:19 says: "We know that we are of God, and that the whole world lies in the power of the evil one." This means Satan and his dark armies of demons can pull strings, tempt people, and lure sinners to do wicked things. Satan hates God, and he uses hate, war, violence, immorality, child abuse, injustice, division, witchcraft, poverty, disease, drugs, alcohol, and idolatry to destroy the people God made. Speaking of Satan, Jesus said: "The thief comes only to steal and kill and destroy" (John 10:10). Satan's kingdom is built on wickedness and absolute evil.

The devil is not all-powerful. God is omnipresent, but the devil doesn't have that kind of influence. Satan cannot be everywhere at one time. Jesus said He saw Satan "fall from heaven like lightning" (Luke 10:18)—referring to the moment when our enemy was cast out of the highest heaven. Satan posts his demons in various regions, but he is not watching us twenty-four hours a day.

Christ has defeated Satan. When Jesus died on the cross, He disarmed satanic powers and made a public spectacle of them (Colossians 2:15). Satan's authority has been taken from him, and all he can do now is lie, steal, kill, and destroy—much like a renegade terrorist army—until the church finishes the job of preaching the gospel to the world. Satan knows his end is near.

Christians have power over demons. Before Jesus ascended into heaven, He announced: "These signs will accompany those who have believed: in My name they will cast out demons" (Mark 16:17). Many times in the Book of Acts we see instances in which followers of Jesus cast out demons. Movies such as *The Exorcist* tried to glorify demons and make them seem all-powerful, but Christians do not have to be afraid of unclean spirits. Demons must leave when we command them to go in the name of Jesus.

The devil will eventually be sentenced to hell. Jesus said hell "has been prepared for the devil and his angels" (Matthew 25:41), and

Revelation 20:10 says after the final judgment God will throw Satan "into the lake of fire and brimstone," where he will be "tormented day and night forever and ever." That is what the devil fears most.

The kingdom of God is so much more powerful than the kingdom of Satan. If you are a believer in Christ, you have no reason to fear the devil. We should not be ignorant of Satan's schemes, and you should develop discernment to know where he is working, but you do not have to be afraid of him. The apostle Paul's words in Romans 16:20 (MEV) remind us of our victory: "The God of peace will soon crush Satan under your feet." We know that one day, because of Christ's victory on the cross, Satan will be forever defeated.

LET'S GO **DEEPER**

1. How is the devil described in Ephesians 2:1–2?

_____

_____

_____

2. Read 2 Corinthians 4:3–4. What is one way that the devil harms people?

_____

_____

_____

3. Read John 8:44. How is Satan described in this passage?

_____

_____

_____

4. How is Satan's kingdom described in Ephesians 6:12?

_____

_____

_____

5. The apostle Paul said we should put on "the full armor of God" to protect ourselves from Satan's attacks. You are not defenseless. God has provided us spiritual weapons to overcome Satan's power. What are the components of this armor, according to Ephesians 6:13–17?

_____

_____

_____

_____

_____

6. Read 2 Corinthians 11:3. What is one way that Satan attacks Christians?

_____

_____

7. How is Satan described in 1 Peter 5:8–9, and how should we respond to his aggressive attacks?

_____

_____

_____

_____

LET'S **TALK** ABOUT IT

Have you ever allowed the devil to influence your life, either through occult practices or other evil things? If so, ask your small group to pray for you.

Memory Verse

Submit therefore to God. Resist the devil and he will flee from you.

—JAMES 4:7

HEROES OF OUR FAITH

JOHN

The Beloved Disciple

In the Gospel that bears his name, John refers to himself as the disciple "whom Jesus loved" (John 13:23). It's possible that he understood who Jesus was better than any human being who ever lived. Along with Peter and James, John was in Jesus' close inner circle. He saw Jesus in all His heavenly glory when Jesus was transfigured on the mountain. While all the other male disciples were scattered and in hiding, John stood at the cross with some of Jesus' brave women followers and witnessed His death. Then, two days later, John went inside Jesus' empty tomb and saw His graveclothes folded up.

On the night before Jesus was crucified, John sat next to Jesus during the Passover meal and laid his head on Jesus' chest. This was probably a normal posture for John because he felt comfortable and secure being close to the Lord. This level of intimacy with Jesus is an example to us all. John taught us how to be passionate followers of Christ.

John's special relationship with Jesus can also be seen at the end of the Bible. After he was banished to the island of Patmos in the Aegean Sea, John had a supernatural vision of the resurrected Jesus that we call "the Revelation." It is the last book of the Bible, and it contains the last words Jesus ever recorded in Scripture. Because John was so close to the Lord, he was trusted to carry this final important message from heaven—which reveals Jesus as the King of all kings and ruler of the universe. John saw Jesus in all His heavenly glory, and he wrote the last amen at the end of the Bible.

The Gift of Eternal Life

What the Bible Says About Heaven and Hell

*"How sweet is rest after fatigue! How sweet will
heaven be when our journey is ended."*
—GEORGE WHITEFIELD (1714-1770)
BRITISH PREACHER AND MISSIONARY TO THE AMERICAN COLONIES

MOST PEOPLE RARELY think about eternity. If they are atheists, they most likely adhere to the theory of evolution. They assume there is no Creator since they see no concrete proof of His existence. They believe human beings slowly evolved from a primordial biological soup and that this world is drifting aimlessly through the galaxies with no purpose and no intelligent designer behind it all. They assume that when people die, their bodies just decompose into meaningless molecules, like all other animals and plants. They scoff at the idea of an afterlife.

Other people may say they believe in life after death, but they focus all their energies on the things of this world. We call them *materialists*. They are in an endless pursuit of worldly success, money, fame, comfort, or pleasure. The only time they dare to think about death is when they attend a funeral—which is a stark and uncomfortable reminder that life is short and material things are fleeting.

Then there are people who believe in reincarnation. They assume that when this life is over, human beings, and even animals, come back to the earth in a different form, perhaps based on their previous behavior. This is the traditional view of Hinduism, but many people who are not Hindus have adopted this as their view. Some people actually undergo "regression therapy" or hypnosis to determine who they were in a past life.

Christians, however, have a very different view of life on this earth. The Bible says life is very short and that when our lives are over we will all face the consequences of our choices. Hebrews 9:27 makes this clear:

> And inasmuch as it is appointed for men to die once and after this comes judgment, so Christ also, having been offered once to bear the sins of many, will appear a second time for salvation without reference to sin, to those who eagerly await Him.

This verse tells us

- we only live and die once—there is no reincarnation,

- after we die, we will face our Creator, and

- those who believe in Christ will be saved from death— which means they will have eternal life.

The Bible also tells us elsewhere that those who reject the mercy of Jesus Christ during their lives on earth will face judgment based on their behavior.

But Christians have a glorious hope of eternal life with God. Author Randy Alcorn puts it this way: "If you're a child of God, you do *not* just 'go around once' on Earth. You don't get just one earthly life. You get another—one far better and without end. You'll inhabit the New Earth! You'll live with the God you cherish and the people you love as an undying person on an undying Earth."[1]

Life is short, and we are to use our time on this earth to serve God and honor Him. The brevity of life is a common theme throughout the Bible. Moses, who lived 120 years and wrote the first five books of the Bible, also wrote the oldest psalm. He said in Psalm 90:10: "As for the days of our life, they contain seventy years, or if due to strength, eighty years, yet their pride is but labor and sorrow; for soon it is gone and we fly away." Other verses in the Bible reveal this common theme:

- "Man is like a mere breath; his days are like a passing shadow" (Psalm 144:4).

- "Behold, you have made my days a few handbreadths, and my lifetime is as nothing before you. Surely all mankind stands as a mere breath!" (Psalm 39:5, ESV).

- "All flesh is like grass and all its glory like the flower of grass. The grass withers, and the flower falls" (1 Peter 1:24, ESV).

While we are living on this earth, God gives us ample opportunity to respond to His love. He offers His blessings to both righteous and unrighteous people, but His desire is for all people to repent of their sins and accept the gift of salvation that was purchased by Jesus. Second Peter 3:9 says: "The Lord is not slow about His promise, as some count slowness, but is patient toward you, not wishing for any to perish but for all to come to repentance." He lovingly offers this gift of eternal life to all, and they have a lifetime to respond, but many people choose to reject it.

LET'S GO **DEEPER**

Christians have several bedrock beliefs about the afterlife that are clearly confirmed in Scripture:

All those people who put their faith in Jesus Christ on this earth will be given the gift of eternal life. Jesus said, "I tell you for certain that everyone who has faith in me has eternal life" (John 6:47, CEV). The apostle Paul wrote, "For the wages of sin is death, but the free gift of God is eternal life in Christ Jesus our Lord" (Romans 6:23). Eternal life actually begins the moment we place our faith in Christ and trust Him to save us. But when we die our spirits will immediately leave our bodies, and we will be ushered into God's presence in heaven.

1. What is one way we can know that we have eternal life, according to 1 John 3:14?

_____

2. Read John 11:26. What does Jesus mean when He says we will "never die"?

_____

_____

People who reject God's mercy will live in the darkness of eternal separation from God. This is not a popular doctrine, but the Bible is painfully clear that people who choose to reject the forgiveness of Christ will be excluded from the benefits and blessings of heaven. They will instead live in eternal separation from God, in a place full of "eternal fire" that is known as hell.

3. Hell was not originally created for people, because God didn't intend for the children He created to go there. Who was hell created for, according to Matthew 25:41?

_____

4. Read 2 Thessalonians 1:6–9. According to verse 8, who are the people who will suffer the judgment of God at the end of time?

_____

_____

_____

5. How is hell described in 2 Thessalonians 1:9?

_____

_____

_____

When Christians die, they immediately go to heaven and live in the presence of God. In the Book of Hebrews, the author describes a scene in heaven where myriads of angels are gathered around the throne of Jesus. In this scene, found in Hebrews 12:22–24, we are told that all those who are "enrolled in heaven" are also standing there. These people are also called "the spirits of the righteous made perfect" (v. 23). In Revelation 15:2–4 these same righteous saints are praising and worshipping God as they stand before His throne.

6. Read Revelation 7:9–12. What is this great multitude of redeemed people doing in heaven?

_____

_____

_____

7. According to 2 Corinthians 5:8, where do Christians go after they die?

_____

_____

When this world ends Jesus will return and establish a new heavenly kingdom here on this earth. Scripture tells us that when it is time for this earth to end, Jesus will return to earth as triumphant King, and all the redeemed saints from years past will come from heaven with Him. Meanwhile those who are alive on earth will be transformed, and all Christians will receive heavenly, glorified bodies.

We will then live in what Revelation 21:1 calls "a new heaven and a new earth." The old world that was stained by sin and wickedness will be burned up, but God will re-create the world to be as it was originally intended. The paradise that Adam and Eve knew, before the curse of sin, will be restored on Planet Earth. Nature will no longer groan under the effects of sin, and all the redeemed saints from all of history will live forever in a world that has no darkness, sickness, wars, violence, tears, or pain.

8. Read 1 John 3:2. What will happen to Christians when Jesus appears for the second time?

_____

_____

9. Read 1 Thessalonians 4:16–17. What is the sequence of events that will happen when Christ returns to earth?

_____

_____

_____

10. Read 1 Corinthians 15:51–53. What will happen to our bodies when Jesus returns to earth?

_____

_____

_____

11. What is the last enemy that Jesus will forever defeat, according to 1 Corinthians 15:54?

_____

One day this dark, sinful world will end and a glorious new earth will become our eternal home. This is the greatest hope we have.

Colossians 3:1 says, "Set your hearts on the things that are in heaven, where Christ sits on his throne" (GNT). Thinking about heaven is not escapism; it is the best kind of therapy. When we feel weary of this world—the corruption, racism, political divisions, viruses, cancer, tyranny, pollution, hatefulness, and injustice—we can remind ourselves that Jesus has defeated death and will one day re-create this world to be the perfect, sinless paradise He always intended for us.

If you are a believer in Jesus, you have the sure promise of a home on the other side. Think about that often; sing about it, and tell everybody else about it.

LET'S **TALK** ABOUT IT

Most people don't like to talk about hell. How would you talk to a non-Christian about the reality of eternal judgment?

Memory Verse

But according to His promise we are looking for new heavens and a new earth, in which righteousness dwells.

—2 PETER 3:13

HEROES OF OUR FAITH

TIMOTHY

A True Spiritual Son

Timothy didn't grow up in Israel, and he never met Jesus personally. He was from a region of Asia Minor called Lycaonia, in what is modern Turkey. His mother was Jewish, and she raised him to respect God and the Scriptures, but his father was Greek. Yet Timothy became a believer in Jesus and began to demonstrate the character of a leader in his local church in a town called Lystra. His faith was so impressive that when the apostle Paul stopped in Lystra to preach, he invited Timothy to travel with him on his missionary journeys. Paul saw a potential successor in this gifted young man.

Timothy proved to be an invaluable companion to Paul, and as he matured he became the apostle's most valued ministry colleague. Of Paul's thirteen epistles, he opens six of them with a greeting from both him and Timothy. And two of Paul's letters were written to Timothy, revealing how much Paul trusted him to share his workload. At one point Paul praises Timothy as his most esteemed disciple: "For I have no one else of kindred spirit who will be concerned for your welfare....But you know of his proven worth, that he served with me in the furtherance of the gospel, like a child serving his father" (Philippians 2:20, 22).

Paul laid hands on Timothy and imparted the Holy Spirit's power to him at some point during his discipleship journey (2 Timothy 1:6), and later Paul sent his spiritual son to pastor the church in Ephesus, a huge city that had become a demonic nest of idolatry and immorality. It was a scary task for a young leader, and Timothy certainly wrestled with fears and doubts. But he had the best of mentors. When Paul was killed, Timothy must have courageously put into practice everything he learned from his spiritual father—and he shared the gospel with the next generation. Paul and Timothy's relationship gives us the best example of how believers in Christ should multiply their influence.

Why Do We Need the Church?

Finding Your Place in God's Family

"When a Christian shuns fellowship with other Christians, the devil smiles."
—Corrie ten Boom (1892-1983)
Dutch Evangelist Who Hid Jews in Her Home During the Nazi Occupation

WHAT COMES TO your mind when someone says the word *church*? You most likely think of a building, perhaps with a steeple, a large cross, a cathedral ceiling, or stained-glass windows. Or maybe you know of a church that meets in a converted store or a former warehouse. But the Bible never refers to the church as a physical building. In fact, most of the small churches that sprang up in the first century, after the resurrection of Jesus, did not have designated buildings. Early Christians met mostly in homes, under trees, in caves, or even in secret underground tunnels.

Before the coming of Jesus, Jews gathered for worship together in buildings called synagogues. So naturally, since many of the earliest Christians came from a Jewish background, the concept of a public meeting to sing hymns and listen to Bible teaching was not a foreign concept. But it would be a few hundred years before Christian church buildings became common. From the beginning of Christianity believers have understood that the church is not a physical structure—it is a tightly knit community of believers who share the same love for Jesus Christ.

After Jesus ascended into heaven His small band of followers met for prayer continually because Jesus had promised to fill them with His Holy Spirit. They prayed for many weeks until one day, on the day of the Jewish harvest festival known as Pentecost, 120 of the disciples were filled, or baptized, with the Spirit, and 3,000 new people were converted to the faith after Peter preached a powerful sermon about Jesus.

Acts 2:41 says that these three thousand new believers were "added" to the number of existing Christians. What were they added to? They were added to the church, the invisible assembly of Christ followers.

The Greek word for *church*, *ekklesia*, is usually translated "the assembled" or "those who are called out."[1] The new converts on the day of Pentecost did not join the church by filling out a card or attending a meeting in a certain building. When they became born-again believers, they were automatically enrolled in the Lord's universal church.

But then they took another step. Acts 2:42 says: "They were continually devoting themselves to the apostles' teaching and to fellowship, to the breaking of bread and to prayer." We don't know exactly where the first Christians did these things, although Acts 2:46 says they were sharing meals "house to house." The important truth we must grasp is that the early church cultivated a strong sense of spiritual community, which they constantly nurtured. They were "continually devoted" to their gatherings. They met for teaching, for prayer, for meals, and to simply spend time with each other. They also were feeding the poor, as well as preaching the gospel everywhere they went.

The word *fellowship*, mentioned in Acts 2:42, is very important because it's the first time this word appears in the Bible. It is the Greek word *koinonia*, and it means "fellowship," "communion," "community," or "intimacy." The word appears roughly nineteen more times in the New Testament to describe the close connection Christian believers share.[2]

Koinonia appears in Acts 2 because this close sense of communion among believers was not possible without the indwelling Holy Spirit. Jesus' death made it possible for the Holy Spirit to live inside believers. And when Christians are together the Holy Spirit in one person connects with the Holy Spirit in another.

This is what Colossians 3:14 calls "the perfect bond of unity." It is the Holy Spirit who connects Christians into tightly knit groups of believers and then into a global church. In a sense, the church is an invisible communion that transcends anything physical, even though we meet in buildings that we own or rent.

This is what makes Christian fellowship so special. No other religion has this unique dynamic. They do not have this invisible bond of the Holy Spirit. Our sense of togetherness is supernatural—and because it originates from the Holy Spirit, it is characterized by a love that can only be described as miraculous. When Jesus was preparing to go to the cross, He told His disciples: "By this all men will know that you are My disciples, if you have love for one another" (John 13:35). The love that Christians have for each other is evidence of the reality of Jesus—it proves He is real!

LET'S GO **DEEPER**

In the New Testament, the church is described in three key ways.

First, the church is a "temple" of the Holy Spirit. First Peter 2:5 says, "You also, as living stones, are being built up as a spiritual house for a holy priesthood, to offer up spiritual sacrifices acceptable to God through Jesus Christ." This verse explains that each individual Christian is a "stone" or "brick" that makes up the spiritual "building" called the church.

The physical building where your church meets is not what's important. What is vital is that we all stay connected to each other, support each other, and work together to create a place where God's presence can be experienced. Just as the temple in the Old Testament was the place where God's glory was manifested, so too God dwells in our midst when we meet together.

1. According to Matthew 18:20, how many people does it require for God's manifest presence to dwell in our midst?

_____

2. Ephesians 2:19–21 celebrates the fact that Gentiles have now been invited to be a part of God's glorious church. They are no longer excluded. In this passage what is the "cornerstone" of God's temple?

_____

3. What is the foundation of this building, according to verse 20?

_____

4. What is the church becoming, according to verse 21?

_____

Second, the church is the "body" of Christ on earth. The apostle Paul often compared the church to a body. He wrote in 1 Corinthians 12:13: "For by one Spirit we were all baptized into one body, whether Jews or Greeks, whether slaves or free, and we were all made to drink of one Spirit."

This verse states that when a person becomes a Christian and receives the Holy Spirit, they immediately become a part of the church and are a member of the "body." This means we each have a role to play in fulfilling the mission of the church on this earth. Verse 27 says it even more plainly: "Now you are Christ's body, and individually members of it."

What an amazing reality—that we as Christians can actually be the hands and feet of Jesus on this earth. He is seated on His throne in heaven, but now His people, who are filled with His Holy Spirit, are representing Jesus to a broken, sinful world that needs His love. We cannot do this individually, but when we are joined together we demonstrate the corporate body of Christ to the community around us.

5. Read Romans 12:4–5. How does the church function since we are made up of so many different people with different abilities?

_____

6. According to Colossians 1:18, who is the head of the church?

_____

Third, the church is a "family" of believers. Ephesians 2:19 says all of us, as believers in Christ, are "family members of the household of God" (TPT). And Romans 12:10 says, "Be kindly affectionate to one another with brotherly love" (NKJV). This means that because we have been supernaturally joined to the church by the Holy Spirit, other Christians are like family members to us. Older men are like fathers; older women are like mothers; we relate to each other as brothers and sisters. This is why you may hear another Christian refer to you as "brother" or "sister."

But now that we are joined into this family, we have some family rules to follow. We have a responsibility to love each other sincerely and do everything we can to foster harmony in our relationships. Throughout the New Testament there are many commandments that relate to our behavior toward each other as Christians. We call these the "one another" verses, and since there are ninety-seven of them, we can't explore them all here. Read these verses and write down how we are commanded to treat each other:

7. Romans 12:10

_____

8. Ephesians 4:32

_____

9. 1 John 3:11

_____

10. Philippians 2:3

_____

11. 1 Peter 5:5

_____

12. 1 Thessalonians 5:11

_____

13. James 5:16

_____

LET'S **TALK** ABOUT IT

Are you involved in a church? If so, what has been the greatest benefit of being connected to a Christian community?

Memory Verse

And let us consider how to stimulate one another to love and good deeds, not forsaking our own assembling together, as is the habit of some, but encouraging one another; and all the more as you see the day drawing near.

—Hebrews 10:24–25

HEROES OF OUR FAITH

CORNELIUS

A Gentile Who Embraced the Gospel

Cornelius was a Roman centurion, which means he commanded a large unit of soldiers. Most likely he had been trained in the art of war by imperial forces in Rome, but he was stationed in the coastal city of Caesarea, the headquarters of the Roman occupation of Judea. Besides the fact that Cornelius was a Gentile, Jews would have avoided this man because he represented everything they hated about their hostile invaders.

And yet Cornelius wasn't hostile to the Jewish people, even though Caesar Augustus was his boss. Probably a wealthy man, Cornelius must have had a noble character because he gave alms to the Jews. Perhaps he was intrigued by their faith. Acts 10:2 says he was "devout," he "feared God," and he "prayed to God continually." He obviously had a humble heart, which explains why God chose him to be an integral part of His plan to reach the nations outside of Israel. An angel appeared to Cornelius, called him by name, and told him to bring the apostle Peter to his home in Caesarea. Cornelius had no idea what message Peter carried, but he sent two servants to the town of Joppa to fetch him.

It was probably very difficult for Peter to enter the house of Cornelius when he arrived, since Jews didn't go inside Gentile homes or eat their food. The wall between Jews and Gentiles was impenetrable in those days. But God had prepared Peter for this moment. Peter preached the gospel to a large group of Cornelius' Italian friends and relatives. And before Peter could finish his sermon, the Gentiles believed in Jesus and began speaking in tongues and praising God. The wall of segregation began crumbling, and the first Gentile church was planted in Israel. From that day on more and more foreigners like Cornelius began to follow Christ all over the Roman Empire and beyond. We honor Cornelius for being a true forerunner of the faith.

LESSON 16

Let's Celebrate the Feast

Why We Take the Lord's Supper

"Come, sinners, to the gospel feast; let every soul be Jesus' guest; ye
need not one be left behind, for God hath bidden all mankind."

—CHARLES WESLEY (1707-1788)
BRITISH REVIVALIST WHO WROTE MORE THAN SIXTY-FIVE HUNDRED HYMNS

CHRISTIANS DON'T BELIEVE rituals or ceremonies save us. The apostle
Paul wrote: "For by grace you have been saved through faith...not
as a result of works" (Ephesians 2:8-9). Yet we practice something regularly called Holy Communion or the Lord's Supper. During this special moment while believers are gathered, everyone eats some bread and
drinks some wine or grape juice to commemorate Jesus' sacrifice on the
cross.

Why do we do this? We must look back to the time of the ancient
Hebrews in Egypt to understand. On the night when God judged Egypt,
a final plague killed the firstborn of every Egyptian family. But God
told the Jews to put lamb's blood on the doorposts of their houses.
Then He promised: "When I see the blood, I will pass over you, and no
plague will befall you to destroy you when I strike the land of Egypt"
(Exodus 12:13). The Hebrews were also told to prepare a special meal of
roasted lamb, unleavened bread, bitter herbs, and wine on that fateful
night.

This meal came to be known among Jews as the Passover because
God "passed over" the houses that were smeared with the lamb's blood.
Anyone who had the blood on his doorpost was spared from death. After
the Hebrews escaped Egypt they were told to celebrate this Passover meal
annually as a way to thank God for His protection.

The Passover was a beautiful preview of what Jesus would do for
us when He died on the cross. Jesus was the perfect "Lamb of God"
(John 1:29), and when we apply His blood by faith to our hearts, God's

judgment "passes over" us and we escape His wrath. People in old covenant times didn't understand this. But now that the Lamb of God has been sacrificed for us, we have a clearer understanding of His mercy.

We are not required to celebrate the Passover meal today (although it is meaningful to participate in one of these dinners to see how it foreshadows the coming of Jesus). God set the old covenant rituals aside, but Jesus instituted something new for us. As He was eating the Passover meal with His disciples on the night before His crucifixion, He took some of the unleavened bread in His hand and said: "This is My body which is given for you" (Luke 22:19). Then He took the cup of wine and said: "This cup which is poured out for you is the new covenant in My blood" (v. 20).

In that moment Jesus totally redefined the Passover meal—and He invited us to join Him in the new celebration. After He shared the bread and wine with His disciples, He gave them some important instructions:

> And when He had taken some bread and given thanks, He broke
> it and gave it to them, saying, "This is My body which is given for
> you; do this in remembrance of Me."
>
> —LUKE 22:19

So we see in this verse that Jesus instructed us to share this bread and wine with each other to remember His sacrifice. The bread represents Jesus' body, which was broken for us. The wine represents His blood, which He spilled to save us. When we partake of the Lord's Supper it is an act of worship; we express our gratitude to Him and honor Him for His great love.

Some Christians use the word *eucharist* for the Lord's Supper. This is from the Greek word *eucharistia*, which means "thanksgiving."[1] When we partake of the bread and wine, we are thanking Jesus for the forgiveness and eternal life He gives us.

When Jesus shared His last Passover meal with His disciples, He said, "Truly I say to you, I will never again drink of the fruit of the vine until that day when I drink it new in the kingdom of God" (Mark 14:25). Jesus was giving us a glimpse of the future when God will host the most mind-blowingly lavish banquet ever prepared.

In the Book of Revelation this feast is called "the marriage supper of the Lamb" (Rev. 19:9, ESV), and it is compared to a marriage feast, which in biblical times lasted several days. It is a glorious banquet designed to honor Jesus, the Bridegroom, and His marriage to the church, which is metaphorically called the bride of Christ. When all redeemed saints are together with Jesus in the new heaven and new earth, we will all attend this party. The Lord's Supper is a preview of what awaits us!

Paul said in 1 Corinthians 5:7–8: "For Christ our Passover also has been sacrificed. Therefore let us celebrate the feast." Even though we only take a small piece of bread and a sip of wine or juice when we take Communion, it is described as a "feast" because of what it represents. It is like a sample, or taste, of the grand gala we will all enjoy at the end of the age. For now our gracious and loving heavenly Father, who loves to host parties, invites us to celebrate our salvation regularly by partaking of Communion.

Some Christians treat the Lord's Supper in a dreary way, with sad religious music and long faces. But this is not a time to be somber. It is not a dead ritual. We are a new covenant people! This is a time to rejoice. Just as you would celebrate Thanksgiving Day with a turkey dinner and pumpkin pies, or enjoy a cake and laughter at a birthday party, Communion is a festive banquet designed to honor and glorify the Savior.

LET'S GO **DEEPER**

1. The apostle Paul gave several instructions about how to celebrate Communion. He quotes Jesus in 1 Corinthians 11:25. How often did Jesus say we are to take Communion?

_____

Some Christians take Communion every week or even more frequently. Others do it less frequently. Jesus gives us liberty in how often we partake. The important thing is that we use the Lord's Supper to remember Him.

2. Read 1 Corinthians 11:26. What do we "proclaim" when we eat the Lord's Supper?

_____

3. Read 1 Corinthians 11:27–30. Paul explains that some people in Corinth were taking Communion in an "unworthy manner." Perhaps the church members did not show reverence for Jesus, or perhaps they were being flippant about it. It is also possible they took the Communion meal without understanding its meaning or that nonbelievers were participating. According to verse 28, what should we do before taking Communion?

_____

_____

_____

It is important to note that only true Christians should partake of Communion, since it is an act of worship and submission to Jesus. If nonbelievers are visiting a church, it is best for them to refrain from taking Communion.

4. Read John 6:53–58. When Jesus spoke about eating His flesh and drinking His blood, He was not speaking literally, of course. This was a reference to the Lord's Supper. When we eat the bread and drink the wine, we honor Jesus as the source of life and salvation. What did Jesus promise those who eat this "bread which came down out of heaven" in verse 58?

_____

LET'S **TALK** ABOUT IT

Take the Lord's Supper together with your small group. Then share why you are grateful for Jesus' sacrifice for you.

Memory Verse

I am the living bread that came down out of heaven; if anyone eats of this bread, he will live forever; and the bread also which I will give for the life of the world is My flesh.

—JOHN 6:51

HEROES OF OUR FAITH

ELIJAH

A Powerful Prophet

Elijah was devoted to God, full of faith, and willing to confront evil no matter the cost. Yet James 5:17 says Elijah was "a man with a nature like ours." He lived seven hundred years before Jesus, and he came from a town in Israel that was so small no one really knows its location. Yet the moment Elijah burst onto the scene and prophesied that God would send a long drought, the wicked King Ahab became terrified of him.

Israel was far from God when Elijah began calling the people to repent and turn from their sins. Ahab had married Jezebel, the daughter of a pagan king, and she was deceptively luring Israel to worship her god, Baal. But Elijah wasn't afraid to challenge Jezebel's sorcery. He invited the whole nation to Mount Carmel, where he gave them a clear choice by asking: "How long will you hesitate between two opinions? If the LORD is God, follow Him; but if Baal, follow him" (1 Kings 18:21). Then Elijah asked God to send heavenly fire to prove He was real. When the fire came down, the people fell on their faces and believed.

Because the Holy Spirit rested upon Elijah so strongly, he performed many miracles. He raised a boy from the dead, prayed for rain after the drought, and watched both flour and oil supernaturally multiply. But the most amazing miracle happened at the end of Elijah's life, when a flaming angelic chariot took him to heaven. Elijah never experienced natural death!

Elijah's miracles were a sort of preview of Jesus' ministry—which explains why some people thought Jesus was Elijah. But Elijah didn't want to be worshipped. When Jesus decided to reveal Himself as the Son of God to His closest disciples, He took them to a mountaintop. There, when the glorious light of heaven began to radiate from Jesus, Elijah and Moses appeared as witnesses to confirm that Jesus is God. (See Matthew 17:1–8.) Elijah stood at Jesus' side to remind us that he, Moses, and all Old Testament heroes had been waiting for the Messiah to arrive. As powerful as Elijah was, he only wanted to be the servant of Christ.

Living in the Overflow

How to Be Filled With the Holy Spirit

"How can we call ourselves a church and not believe in healing and in miracles? I cannot read four pages anywhere in the Bible without encountering miracles! And the God of the Bible is the same today!"
—T. L. OSBORN (1923-2013)
PENTECOSTAL EVANGELIST WHO PREACHED IN SEVENTY COUNTRIES

M ANY CENTURIES BEFORE the coming of Jesus, the prophet Joel pre-dicted that a time would come in history when the Holy Spirit would be "poured out" on people from every nation and ethnicity. He said, "I will pour out My Spirit on all mankind; and your sons and daughters will prophesy" (Joel 2:28). This was a revolutionary prophecy for many reasons. First, in the Old Testament period only Jews enjoyed the benefits of God's favor and blessing; and second, the Holy Spirit did not live inside of people in that era.

The Old Testament speaks of the Holy Spirit "coming upon" people in those days. God would sometimes anoint special people to serve Him—such as prophets, kings, priests, or warriors—but average people did not have access to this blessing. So for Joel to predict that men, women, young, old, rich, and poor could experience the power of the Holy Spirit was a radical proposal.

But this is exactly what happened after Jesus paid for our sins. He made it possible for the Holy Spirit to make His abode inside of all believers. Jesus constantly reminded His disciples that when He left this earth He would send His Holy Spirit to comfort, guide, and strengthen us. He even went so far as to say that the Holy Spirit's presence would be better than Him being with them in person. Jesus said in John 16:7:

> But I tell you the truth, it is to your advantage that I go away; for
> if I do not go away, the Helper will not come to you; but if I go, I
> will send Him to you.

For that reason the first disciples had a sense of expectation about what would happen after Jesus ascended to heaven. What could possibly be better than having Jesus right there with them, in the flesh? How could it be better if He went away? Jesus had promised "the Helper"—the Holy Spirit. But what would that be like? Jesus had a big surprise for them.

Right before Jesus ascended, Jesus told His followers: "And behold, I am sending forth the promise of My Father upon you; but you are to stay in the city until you are clothed with power from on high" (Luke 24:49). When Jesus said the phrase "clothed with power," His disciples would have recognized a reference to the story of Elijah. That one dramatic miracle convinced the nation of Israel that Jehovah was the true God.

Elijah was an unusual character because he did not die a natural death. He was taken into heaven supernaturally. The Bible says that right before this miracle his disciple Elisha asked if he could have a double portion of his power. Elijah told Elisha that this would be difficult, but he did not deny the request. So when heaven's fiery chariots came to sweep Elijah into glory, he threw his mantle, or robe, on Elisha—signifying that Elisha was now "clothed" with new and special grace. If you continue reading the story, you learn that Elisha performed twice as many miracles as his mentor.

This is essentially what Jesus did for His church. After He was taken to heaven Jesus poured out His Holy Spirit on the church so that we could do the same miracles He did. Jesus did not leave us on this earth without the supernatural ability to fulfill His mission. He gave us His mantle. He gave us power and authority, and it all came through the Holy Spirit.

So the disciples of Jesus did exactly what Jesus commanded. They did not leave Jerusalem, even though they were excited to tell everyone about His resurrection. They waited to be clothed with power. They didn't know what this would look like. They simply had an expectation, mixed with great faith.

Several weeks later the miracle happened. Jesus had not given them a specific time for the Holy Spirit's powerful visitation. But on the day of

Pentecost, while 120 of His disciples were praying in an upper room in Jerusalem, they were startled. Acts 2:2–4 says:

> And suddenly there came from heaven a noise like a violent rushing wind, and it filled the whole house where they were sitting. And there appeared to them tongues as of fire distributing themselves, and they rested on each one of them. And they were all filled with the Holy Spirit and began to speak with other tongues, as the Spirit was giving them utterance.

They heard the sound of a wind, but it was not a normal or natural wind. It was the wind of the Holy Spirit. They saw flames of fire on each other's heads, but this was not normal or natural fire. It was the fire of the Spirit, who grants us heavenly power. And suddenly they received a strange ability to speak in languages they didn't know. The Holy Spirit was filling them with an uncanny ability to become witnesses for Jesus to the whole world.

Can you see why Jesus did not want them to preach His message before they had this power? They would have had to rely on their own intellect, and they would have been limited by their timidity. Yet because they waited, a holy fire filled their hearts and they had the boldness and supernatural grace to fulfill God's plan, and to do it His way.

This is God's plan for every Christian. He wants you to rely fully on His Holy Spirit, not on your brainpower, your good ideas, or your natural talents. God wants us to be saturated, or clothed, with His power. The church cannot do its job if we are filled with ourselves; we must be empty and surrendered so God can work.

LET'S GO **DEEPER**

1. Jesus gave His disciples plenty of advance warning that they would be filled with the Holy Spirit. To what did He compare the Holy Spirit in John 7:38?

2. Jesus promised in Mark 16:17–18 that His followers would have access to supernatural power. What miracles did Jesus say would follow those who believe in Him?

_____

_____

_____

3. Just before Jesus ascended into heaven, what did He tell His disciples would happen to them in Acts 1:5?

_____

(Note: This word *baptized* is the same word used for water baptism, but baptism in the Holy Spirit is different. Just as we are fully submerged in water when we are baptized, we are fully submerged or saturated in the Holy Spirit when He fills us. God does not want us to have just a small amount of the Spirit—He wants to fully soak us in the Spirit!)

4. The disciples were again "filled with the Holy Spirit" in Acts 4:31, probably because there were new Christians in this group who were not in the prayer meeting on the day of Pentecost. What happened when these disciples were filled with the Spirit?

_____

_____

_____

5. The apostle Peter eventually preached to a group of Gentiles in Caesarea, and they were filled with the Holy Spirit while he was speaking. What happened to them in Acts 10:44–46?

_____

_____

6. The apostle Paul and all other New Testament believers relied on the Holy Spirit's power, and this is why they saw miracles as they preached. What was the secret of Paul's power, according to 1 Corinthians 2:4?

_____

_____

_____

7. Based on Ephesians 5:18, what is the secret to a powerful Christian life?

_____

LET'S **TALK** ABOUT IT

Have you had the experience of being filled with the Holy Spirit? If not, would you like other group members to pray for you now?

Memory Verse

But you will receive power when the Holy Spirit comes on you; and you will be my witnesses in Jerusalem, and in all Judea and Samaria, and to the ends of the earth.

—Acts 1:8, esv

LET'S GO EVEN DEEPER
You Can Pray for the Baptism of the Holy Spirit

Based on what we have learned so far, there are really two major experiences every Christian needs. One is salvation, which we have already explained in detail. The second is the baptism of the Holy Spirit, or what is also called the infilling of the Holy Spirit. Every Christian receives the Holy Spirit when they are born again. But after salvation we need to be saturated in the Holy Spirit's power so that we can effectively minister to the people around us.

Sadly, some Christians are satisfied to have the Holy Spirit's presence in their lives, but they don't really want His power. They want to enjoy the benefits of His comfort, His gentle guidance, and His revelation from Scripture, but they don't want to preach to other people, heal the sick, cast out demons, or use the miraculous power Jesus has made available to us. They feel comfortable in the shallow water and don't want to venture into the deep.

I hope you want the fullness of the Spirit in your life! When we have this experience the Holy Spirit's power fills us so full that He overflows like a mighty waterfall. Also, when we are baptized in the Spirit, unusual gifts of the Holy Spirit—which are listed in 1 Corinthians 12:8–10—begin to be manifested in our lives. We begin to experience His supernatural power. These gifts include prophecy, miracles, healing, and speaking in unknown languages. (We will study more about this in lesson 22.)

Being baptized in the Holy Spirit is not something you have to qualify for. Any Christian can ask for it, and Jesus is ready to do it. You can pray by yourself, or you can ask someone else to pray for you. Here are the simple steps you can take to be filled with the Holy Spirit:

1. Prepare your heart. The Holy Spirit is holy. He is compared to a fire (Matthew 3:11), which means He purifies sin and burns up what is not Christlike in our lives. Make sure you have confessed all known sin and made your heart ready for His infilling.

2. Ask Jesus to baptize you in the Holy Spirit. You do not jump through hoops to get God's attention. He is eager to answer your request. Jesus is the one who baptizes us in the Spirit—so ask Him, and use your faith. Expect Him to answer.

3. Receive the infilling. Begin to thank Him for this miracle. The Holy Spirit's power is filling your life. If you feel your mind is clouded with doubts, just praise the Lord. Focus your mind on Him and not on yourself.

4. Release your prayer language. The moment people are filled with the Holy Spirit, they often receive the ability to speak in a heavenly language—just as the disciples did on the day of Pentecost. You may feel the words bubbling up inside of you. You may hear the words in your mind. Open your mouth and begin to speak, trusting the Lord to cause His power to overflow in you. And if you don't receive your prayer language immediately, stand in faith knowing that the Lord has already filled you. God does things according to His timetable, not ours.

5. Step out in boldness. After you have been filled with the Spirit, one of the first things you will notice is a new boldness to talk with others about Jesus. The Holy Spirit wants you to be a courageous witness. Psalm 107:2 says, "Let the redeemed of the LORD say so." When the doors open and you find yourself in a conversation with someone who doesn't know God, rely on the Holy Spirit to give you the confidence to tell them all about what Jesus has done for us.

HEROES OF OUR FAITH

JEREMIAH

He Wept for Sinners

We tend to think of Old Testament prophets as angry men who shook their fists and declared harsh words of judgment. It's true that prophets say unpopular things—because God requires them to confront bad behavior. But in the case of Jeremiah, he took no delight in chastising Israel for her many sins. In fact, he often wept as he told his fellow Jews that God would destroy their nation if they didn't repent. He cried out: "Oh that my head were waters and my eyes a fountain of tears, that I might weep day and night for the slain of the daughter of my people!" (Jeremiah 9:1).

The son of a Jewish priest, Jeremiah lived six hundred years before Jesus. God called him to be a prophet when he was just a young man. Because his message was so confrontational, his family turned against him, he was ridiculed, he was beaten and thrown in jail, he was threatened by one of Judah's kings, and he was even thrown into the bottom of a well. No one wanted to hear what Jeremiah had to say, yet he kept on saying it. God gave him supernatural courage.

Even though Jeremiah constantly warned the Jews about the awful consequences of sin, he also brought a message of hope. God always offers forgiveness if we repent. But Israel didn't listen—so Jeremiah prophesied that they would end up as slaves in a foreign land for seventy years. And that's exactly what happened. The Babylonians invaded Israel and destroyed the Jewish temple. And the Israelites were dragged to Babylon, where they were captives for seventy years.

Even though Jeremiah's life was sad and full of rejection, he saw a bright future over the horizon. God showed him a glorious day, six hundred years into the future, when He would institute the new covenant through Jesus Christ. Jeremiah predicted that God would abolish the old covenant system, which required people to perfectly follow God's laws in their own ability. God told Jeremiah: "I will put My law within them and on their heart I will write it" (Jeremiah 31:33). This is exactly what God did after Jesus died on the cross for us.

LESSON 18

Becoming Close to Jesus

How to Pursue Intimacy With the Lord

"The more we know Him, the more we will desire to know
Him. As love increases with knowledge, the more we know
God, the more we will truly love Him. We will learn to love
Him equally in times of distress or in times of great joy."

—BROTHER LAWRENCE (1614-1691)
FRENCH LAY MONK WHOSE SIMPLE TEACHINGS WERE COMPILED IN A BOOK,
THE PRACTICE OF THE PRESENCE OF GOD, PUBLISHED AFTER HIS DEATH

MOST RELIGIONS IN the world involve following a specific list of rituals, obeying a list of rules or strict belief in certain creeds. For example, Muslims are expected to pray five times a day, facing east in the direction of Saudi Arabia. Hindus are expected to give food offerings to the idols of their gods or to bathe in a specific river to be cleansed from their sins. Orthodox Jews in Israel are very careful not to do any work on Saturdays because it is the official Sabbath when rest is required.

But Christianity is different. You will often hear followers of Jesus say this: "Christianity is not a religion—it is a relationship." In all other world religions, people approach God with caution, and they serve Him from a distance—without any assurance that God actually loves them or accepts them. This is what makes the Christian faith so different from all other religious beliefs. The Bible teaches us that God wants to know us and that He desires a close, intimate relationship with us.

Jesus defined this when He invited His disciples to be His "friends." He told them in John 15:15:

> No longer do I call you slaves, for the slave does not know what his master is doing; but I have called you friends, for all things that I have heard from My Father I have made known to you.

Jesus was emphasizing here that He does not want to relate to us as a master relates to slaves, or as a boss relates to employees. He does not want a cold, impersonal connection with us, where we simply submit and follow orders. Yes, He is our Lord, and He is our ultimate authority—but He wants a warm, affectionate friendship. He invites us to know the Father, Son, and Holy Spirit in unimaginable closeness.

Of all the original disciples, the apostle John probably had the closest friendship with Jesus. He watched Jesus die on the cross, he saw Jesus after He was raised from the dead, and then he had glorious visions of the resurrected Savior when he was in exile. And John wrote these words to all of us in 1 John 1:3:

> What we have seen and heard we proclaim to you also, so that you too may have fellowship with us; and indeed our fellowship is with the Father, and with His Son Jesus Christ.

John was saying, "You can have the same closeness to Jesus that we have!" God invites us into what John calls "fellowship." As we have stated earlier in this study, the Greek word for *fellowship* is *koinonia*, which can be translated as "communion, joint participation, or intimacy."[1] We can have a deep and abiding connection with God because of what Jesus did for us when He paid for our sins. We don't have to work, pay money, pass a test, or follow a list of rules to be friends with God. We simply believe in Him, and then we can rest in His love. We can, in essence, relax in His arms and let Him cuddle us like a father would his children.

I've met only a few people who didn't know who their father is. But I often meet people who doubt God loves them as a father. The Bible tells us that when we are born again, the Holy Spirit enters our hearts to solve our own paternity mystery. Romans 8:15 says, "You have received a spirit of adoption as sons by which we cry out, 'Abba! Father!'" This means God has literally adopted you to become His own child. The Holy Spirit helps us understand who we belong to. And His name is "Abba"—the Hebrew word for Daddy or Papa.

Are you uncomfortable calling God your Daddy? If you are, you really don't believe Romans 8:15. He is Abba! The problem is that many people believe God is very distant, always angry, and too busy managing heaven to take notice of us. That's how the legalistic Pharisees viewed God, but Jesus challenged their warped ideas.

Throughout His life on earth, Jesus showed us that God is approachable, accepting of all people, friendly toward sinners, forgiving, protective, and affectionate. He even let the disciple John lay his head on His chest (John 13:23)—something a proper Pharisee would never do. Yet Jesus isn't the slightest bit religious. If you allow Him, He will pull you close to His chest and let you hear the beating of His heart. He really wants you to be close!

When some people hear the word *father*, it conjures up painful memories of domestic abuse, abandonment, alcoholism, or frightening punishments. Others associate "father" with a numb detachment—because they never connected emotionally with their dads. These are called "father wounds," and these hurts can be caused by mothers too. Let the Holy Spirit heal you of these wounds so He can show you that your heavenly Daddy is strong, compassionate, accepting, gentle, kind, and faithful.

If you want to develop a close, intimate relationship with the Lord, make sure you have fully accepted the forgiveness of Christ. Many people keep God at a distance because they assume He's still mad at them for their past sins. But the Bible says He does not even remember our sins— He casts them "into the depths of the sea" (Micah 7:19). God did not halfheartedly or reluctantly forgive you; He forgave you from His gushing heart of love. Yes, it was a legal transaction, but it was enacted out of a wondrous compassion that will take all of eternity to comprehend.

The Bible says God directed all His righteous anger toward Jesus and laid our punishment on Him—so that He could remove the barrier that separated us. All because of love! He is not angry at you now. He loves you so much He actually threw a party to welcome you into His presence. He doesn't just tolerate you; He delights in you!

An early church leader known as Augustine, who lived in the fourth century, wrote: "To fall in love with God is the greatest of all romances; to seek him, the greatest adventure; to find him, the greatest human achievement."[2] You are invited to experience this adventure.

If you've ever had a romantic relationship with a person who eventually became your spouse, you know that true love can make you do crazy things. When you love a person, you want to spend lots of time with them, you want to buy them gifts, you might write them love letters. You might even write them a song or a poem.

The same thing can happen in your relationship with God. Once you know His love for you is this amazing, you will respond by pursuing Him in many different ways:

- You will want to spend time with Him privately.

- You will want to read the Bible, which is His love letter to us.

- You will want to listen to worship music, which draws your heart closer to Him, and you will want to sing to Him as well.

- You will want to learn more about Him by listening to sermons at church or video teachings online or by attending Bible studies.

- And you will want to obey Him and honor Him in every area, avoiding sin because you want to please Him.

As you become a pursuer of God, your devotion to Him will intensify. This is the heart of the Christian life.

LET'S GO **DEEPER**

1. In Mark 12:30 Jesus quoted the Old Testament to explain how intensely we should love God. How did Jesus say we should love God?

_____

_____

_____

2. Read John 17:3. What is true life really all about?

_____

_____

_____

3. King David wrote many psalms about his passionate love for God. What did this intense love compel David to do in Psalm 63:1?

_____

_____

4. What is the main reason that we love God, according to 1 John 4:19?

_____

5. Read Jeremiah 29:12–13. What does God promise to those who seek the Lord intensely?

_____

_____

_____

6. The prophet Hosea calls us to "press on to know the LORD" in Hosea 6:3. What does the prophet say will happen if we do this?

_____

LET'S **TALK** ABOUT IT

Is there anything that is keeping you from getting closer to Jesus? Shame? Fear? Apathy? Share from your heart, and allow others to pray for you.

Memory Verse

Behold, I stand at the door and knock; if anyone hears My voice and opens the door, I will come in to him and will dine with him, and he with Me.

—REVELATION 3:20

HEROES OF OUR FAITH

SILAS

He Served Faithfully in the Background

The first time we read about Silas, in Acts 15:22, we learn that he was sent by the apostles to the city of Antioch to serve alongside Paul and Barnabas. He showed great leadership potential in the early church. He traveled with Paul to Syria, Corinth, Berea, Thessalonica, and other regions—yet he is never quoted in Scripture. He is always mentioned as accompanying Paul, Peter, Timothy, or other leaders. Also known as Silvanus ("Silas" may have been a nickname or a Greek version of his name), he was obviously a team player. He wasn't hungry for attention or applause. He didn't mind being someone else's support.

We see his willingness to help others on the team in 1 Peter 5:12, where Peter praises Silvanus because he served as a scribe by writing down Peter's first epistle. Silvanus was not the author of 1 Peter, but he wrote it down with his own pen as he listened to Peter's dictation. Peter calls Silvanus "our faithful brother." Silvanus' faithfulness is equally evident in 2 Corinthians 1:19, where Paul tells us that he, Silvanus, and Timothy all preached the gospel to the people in Corinth. And when Paul wrote his two epistles to the Thessalonians, he addressed both letters from "Paul and Silvanus and Timothy." It might seem that Silvanus was always in the background, but this doesn't minimize his efforts to plant the seed of the gospel.

Perhaps the most remarkable story about Silas occurred when he and Paul were arrested and beaten with rods in Philippi after Paul cast a demon out of a slave girl. The two brave men were chained to the floor of a prison, but they began to sing praises to God in the middle of the night. Suddenly an earthquake shook the building, all the doors flung open, and all their chains fell off. Paul and Silas then led the jailer to salvation and baptized him and his family. (See Acts 16:25-34.) Silas learned that when we sing praises in our worst moments, God does miracles. Silas worked hard for the Lord, and he probably suffered much hardship, but he sang with joy in spite of bleak circumstances. May we learn from his humble example!

This Is Why We Sing

Cultivating a Life of Worship

"In the end, worship can never be a performance, something you're pretending or putting on. It's got to be an overflow of your heart.... Worship is about getting personal with God, drawing close to God."

—MATT REDMAN (1974–)
BRITISH WORSHIP LEADER AND SONGWRITER

CHRISTIANS LOVE TO sing. No matter where in the world they live, believers in Jesus typically worship for twenty, thirty, or forty minutes each time they meet together. Music styles vary; some churches sing older hymns accompanied only by a piano, while contemporary churches have many singers on the stage along with guitars, bass guitars, and drums. In poorer countries worshippers may use drums made of animal skins while a choir sings a cappella; in developed countries churches may have elaborate sound systems with projectors to show the lyrics on a screen.

But regardless of race, culture, class, or denomination, music that exalts and glorifies God is a huge part of the Christian life. When we sing we give God the honor, glory, thanks, and praise He deserves. We sing about His majesty, His mercy, His power, and His love—and we worship with deep passion and overflowing gratitude. Our songs also remind us who God is, and they help us connect deeply with Him.

Why is praise and worship so central to our faith? If you look in the exact middle of your Bible you'll find the Book of Psalms, the ancient hymnbook of the Jewish people. It contains 150 songs that were used for centuries to celebrate God's goodness, love, and mercy. Just as the psalms are in the middle of the Scriptures, praise is at the core of everything we believe. Many of the words in the psalms are used in modern songs today, and people have written thousands of new songs to honor and exalt the Lord.

True worship is more or less like singing love songs to God. It is our feeble attempt to tell God how much we love Him. King David, who was a skilled musician, wrote at least 73 of the 150 love songs in Scripture. He and other anonymous musicians articulated what it means to have a relationship with God.

Musical styles have changed much since King David's era, but Christians have continued to praise and worship God joyfully and passionately through the ages. Some of the greatest songs, concertos, operas, ballads, or anthems ever written, in fact, could be classified as worship music. Just as Christians *pray*, Christians also *praise*. We are a worshipping people. Here are five things that will help you make worship the core of your life:

1. Praise and worship attracts God's manifest presence. James 4:8 says, "Draw near to God and He will draw near to you." When we humble ourselves before God and sing about His love for us, He responds. This happens when we're alone, but it also happens when we worship together corporately.

Jesus also taught that the Father seeks people to be His worshippers if they worship "in spirit and truth" (John 4:23). God wants our worship to be sincere, not fake or with wrong motives. Worship is sometimes compared to incense in the Bible. If our worship is honest, heartfelt, and authentic, the Lord will receive it as a sweet-smelling aroma that brings Him great pleasure.

2. Praise and worship focuses our hearts and minds on God. Psalm 92:4 says, "For You, O Lord, have made me glad by what You have done, I will sing for joy at the works of Your hands." Singing about God's goodness, His power, His majesty, and His love causes us to take our eyes off our problems. Singing about Him quells our fears, inspires our faith, and rekindles our joy. Worship is like medicine to a heavy heart.

3. Praise and worship honors God. First Chronicles 16:23–24 says: "Sing to the Lord, all the earth; proclaim good tidings of His salvation from day to day. Tell of His glory among the nations." God doesn't need our praise. But when we praise Him it honors Him among the people so they can turn to Him. Christian music, whether it's sung in a church, played on the radio, or performed at a concert, points people to heaven.

4. Praise and worship defeats our enemies. It's difficult to understand how our singing affects Satan's kingdom because the impact is invisible. But when we praise God He responds by defeating His enemies. In the

Old Testament God told King Jehoshaphat to send the singers out in front of Israel's army. When they began worshipping, the Lord set ambushes against the hostile enemy army (2 Chronicles 20:22). If you are facing a crisis, your best response is to sing praises to God.

5. Praise and worship should be done with exuberance. British preacher John Wesley (1703–1791) hated lukewarm worship. He told his followers: "Beware of singing as if you were half dead, or half asleep; but lift up your voice with strength."[1] The Book of Psalms never endorses half-hearted worship. Psalm 86:12 says, "I will give thanks to You, O Lord my God, *with all my heart*" (emphasis added). When we praise God with total surrender we are more likely to embrace His will for our lives completely. Your goal is to learn to worship with all your heart.

LET'S GO **DEEPER**

King David instructed people to worship God in some specific ways. Read these verses and list the different ways we express our devotion to the Lord:

1. Psalm 96:1–2

_____

2. Psalm 100:1

_____

3. Psalm 47:1

_____

4. Psalm 5:7

_____

5. Psalm 95:6

---

6. Psalm 149:3

---

7. Read Psalm 63:1. If we want to worship God wholeheartedly, what attitude must we have?

---

8. Read Psalm 63:3–4. How long should we praise God?

---

9. Read Psalm 34:1. When should we bless and praise God?

The last psalm in the Bible, Psalm 150, is a noisy musical climax of trumpets, harps, stringed instruments, and different types of cymbals. It is like a huge exclamation point at the end of the book, calling all people to praise God—not only in the church (the "sanctuary") but also in the world. It reminds us that at the end of time all creation will celebrate the goodness of God and acknowledge His loving authority.

The word *hallelujah* appears three times in this psalm, once in verse 1 and twice in verse 6. Hallelujah is a Hebrew word that means "Praise the Lord," and Christians all over the world use this word in their worship to express their heartfelt adoration to God. It is a word that unites Christians globally. This word should become a part of your vocabulary now, if it isn't already.

10. Revelation 19:4–6 shows us a glimpse of what redeemed people will be doing at the end of time. How does it describe the scene as this multitude stands near God's throne? What are the saints saying?

_____

_____

_____

One day all Christians will stand in the presence of almighty God and bow before the glorious Lamb of God, Jesus Christ. We will forever worship Him and praise Him for redeeming us. All the praise we give Him now, on this side of eternity, is simply preparation for eternal life with Him forever.

LET'S **TALK** ABOUT IT

Do you feel comfortable praising God in a public church meeting? Why is it important to worship God wholeheartedly?

Memory Verse

Serve the LORD with gladness; come before Him with joyful singing.

—PSALM 100:2

HEROES OF OUR FAITH

JAMES

A Brother of Jesus Who Believed

Can you imagine what it would have been like to grow up in the home of Joseph and Mary, the parents of Jesus? The Bible lists four brothers of Jesus—James, Joseph, Simon, and Judas (or "Jude")—along with some unnamed sisters, in Matthew 13:55-56. Did these siblings know that Jesus was the Son of God? It's likely that Mary would have shared the story of the virgin birth with them, but during the three and a half years of Jesus' ministry on earth, James didn't believe in His divinity. Perhaps he was too close to Jesus to accept this wild idea that the boy he shared a room with growing up was the Son of God!

All this changed after Jesus' resurrection. The apostle Paul tells us in 1 Corinthians 15:7 that Jesus appeared to James after He showed His pierced hands and feet to His close followers. His brother had not seen the many healings Jesus had performed; he didn't see the food multiplied for the multitude, the resurrection of Lazarus, or the many exorcisms Jesus performed. James may have even scoffed at Jesus when he heard about these miracles. Yet when he saw his brother alive after He had been in the tomb for three days, James became a strong believer. He was a late adapter, but that did not disqualify James from becoming a part of Jesus' team.

James must have grown quickly as a disciple because he became a leader in the early church. Paul calls him a pillar of the church in Galatians 2:9, and when the early Jewish Christians struggled with the idea of Gentiles joining their movement, James advised them to open their hearts to this radical new idea. James also wrote part of the Bible, and the short epistle that bears his name contains the word *faith* sixteen times. How amazing that this man who doubted that Jesus was God in the beginning became a champion of Christian faith later in his life. This should encourage us all that even if we had doubts in the beginning, we can become strong believers!

Fighting the Good Fight

How to Resist Temptation

"There is a charm about the forbidden that makes it unspeakably desirable."
—MARK TWAIN (1835–1910)
WRITER AND HUMORIST KNOWN AS THE FATHER OF AMERICAN LITERATURE

ONE OF THE fastest-growing categories of books on the market today is the self-help genre. There are millions of titles designed to teach people how to start a business, manage a company, become emotionally healthy, maintain friendships, and of course lose weight, stop smoking, or improve their sex lives. But you probably won't find a book on the market called *How to Stop Sinning*. The reason is simple: it is impossible for human beings to stop sinning on their own. Self-help will not provide the answers.

Everyone knows this, regardless of their spiritual condition. Prince, the pop singer who sold more than 150 million records before his untimely death, once sang about always wanting to do what's wrong.[1] Irish poet Oscar Wilde admitted, "The only way to get rid of temptation is to yield to it."[2] And 1930s Hollywood star Mae West was really not joking when she said, "Between two evils, I always pick the one I never tried before."[3]

Some people assume that when a person becomes a Christian they stop struggling with temptation. That is not true! A person may repent of their known sins, put their faith in Jesus, and experience a miraculous conversion—but when they wake up the next day they will realize they might still sometimes feel anger, say unkind words, or think impure thoughts.

People who are addicted to drugs, alcohol, pornography, or gambling can discover the forgiveness of Christ, but they may not immediately overcome all their bad habits overnight. And when they do stop these harmful habits they may feel tempted to return to them. They must learn to resist temptation with the help of the indwelling Holy Spirit.

The apostle Paul wrote some masterful words about this dilemma in his letter to the Romans. Even though Paul was a spiritual giant and a theological genius, he admits that he too felt weak when he faced the attraction of sin. Paul wrote in Romans 7:18–21 that as long as we are in this body on this side of eternity, sin maintains a pull on us:

> For I know that nothing good dwells in me, that is, in my flesh; for the willing is present in me, but the doing of the good is not. For the good that I want, I do not do, but I practice the very evil that I do not want. But if I am doing the very thing I do not want, I am no longer the one doing it, but sin which dwells in me. I find then the principle that evil is present in me, the one who wants to do good.

Paul is not talking here about the struggle of a person before conversion. He is describing our faith journey after we give our hearts to Christ. Even though we love the Lord, and the Holy Spirit lives in us, we have a battle on our hands. We have what Paul describes as a "sinful nature," and it constantly rages. Our flesh wants to disobey the law of God even though our awakened conscience wants to do what is right. We all face this conflict.

Some people, for example, feel frustrated and discouraged because they end up looking at pornography, even though they hate it and despise the guilt they feel after looking at it. The attraction of sin becomes even more difficult because pornography is easily accessible and because so many people around us are living in immoral relationships in a culture that celebrates sexual sin. This was certainly true for the people Paul was writing to in ancient Rome.

What is the key to victory over temptation? Let's imagine you live in a two-story house with a basement. You rarely go down to the lowest level of the house because you know there is a caged monster down there. It has fangs, claws, and a hideous appearance. You can hear it growling every day, and you know it is vicious.

This monster cannot attack you because it is in a locked cage. All it can do is scare you—unless, of course, you decide to venture into the basement and stick your hands between the bars of the cage. Or, if you want to be really stupid, you can take the key hanging on the wall, open the cage, and give it some food. You will then become its victim.

What is the solution? You must ignore the monster. And it would be easier to ignore its growling if you remained on the top floor of the house, as far away from the noise as possible. The monster is still there, but if you are so far above it that you can't hear its menacing cries, you will never go near it.

This is essentially what the apostle Paul told the Romans to do with their sin nature. First he asked an obvious question: "Wretched man that I am! Who will set me free from the body of this death?" (Romans 7:24). Then he provided the answer:

> Thanks be to God through Jesus Christ our Lord! So then, on the one hand I myself with my mind am serving the law of God, but on the other, with my flesh the law of sin. Therefore there is now no condemnation for those who are in Christ Jesus. For the law of the Spirit of life in Christ Jesus has set you free from the law of sin and of death.
>
> —ROMANS 7:25–8:2

Paul calls us higher, to a place of escape. Although we will never be completely free from the pull of sin in this life, God gives us, through the new covenant of grace, a means to drown out the sound of the monster in our basement. When we do this the Bible says we are "walking in the Spirit" rather than fulfilling the desire of the flesh.

If you are struggling with a sinful habit or a constant temptation, or if you have fallen into the same sin multiple times and feel like a failure, leave the "basement" and climb to the top level of your house. Take your position with the resurrected Christ, who has defeated sin.

As you plant your feet firmly above the monster of your sin nature, meditate on the truth of Paul's words in Romans 6:14: "For sin shall not be master over you, for you are not under law but under grace." Christ lives in you, and His grace has been given to you in this conflict. You can look down on the raging monster of sin and tell it to be quiet.

LET'S GO **DEEPER**

1. Read Ephesians 2:4-6. After Christ died for us, made us alive with Him, and raised us with Him, where were we seated?

_____

2. Read Romans 8:1-2. What has "the law of the Spirit of life in Christ Jesus" done for us?

_____

We can compare this "law of the Spirit of life in Christ Jesus" mentioned in Romans 8:2 to the law of aerodynamics. We know there is a law of gravity, but the law of aerodynamics is more powerful than gravity. A giant Airbus A340 full of people, and loaded with fuel, weighs 820,000 pounds—and yet because of the law of aerodynamics, it can fly above the earth. You also can "soar" above sin even though that sin normally would drag you down to earth. This is the miracle of grace!

3. Read 1 Corinthians 10:13. What does God promise to provide for us when we are tempted?

_____

4. Read James 1:13-15. What is the true cause of temptation?

_____

Hebrews 4:15 says Jesus was "tempted in all things," and yet He did not sin. This should bring us great comfort that Jesus—because He was fully man and also fully God—understood our human temptations.

5. Read Matthew 4:4, 7, and 10. What did Jesus say to the devil to resist his temptations?

_____

6. Read Galatians 5:16–18. What is the simple secret to avoiding the desires of the flesh?

_____

7. Read Galatians 5:24. What is said about those people who belong to Christ Jesus?

_____

LET'S **TALK** ABOUT IT

Share about a time in your life when you were able to overcome a specific temptation.

Memory Verse

Keep watching and praying that you may not enter into temptation; the spirit is willing, but the flesh is weak.

—MATTHEW 26:41

HEROES OF OUR FAITH

HANNAH

She Taught Us to Pray

When we first meet Hannah in the Bible she is a very sad woman. She couldn't have children, and her infertility was made worse by the fact that her husband was polygamous—and the other wife taunted Hannah for her barrenness. Yet because Hannah loved God she didn't lash out at people because of her painful circumstances. She prayed to God for a child—and in the end she not only had a son, Samuel, but three more sons and two daughters.

God honored Hannah for her great faith. Even though she was depressed, she went to the place of worship in Ramah, where she "prayed to the LORD and wept bitterly" (1 Samuel 1:10). The Jewish priest Eli accused her of being drunk because of her passionate praying, but Hannah held fast to her faith. When her baby, Samuel, was born, she dedicated him to the Lord, and he became a powerful prophet in Israel. Samuel eventually anointed King David to rule the nation.

In those dark days women suffered unimaginable abuse and injustice. And yet God honored Hannah, and her inspired song of thanksgiving became part of the Bible (1 Samuel 2:1–10). In this prophetic declaration Hannah actually prophesied about the coming of Jesus, the Messiah. She said: "Those who contend with the LORD will be shattered...and He will give strength to His king, and will exalt the horn of His anointed" (v. 10). Hannah's story shows us that God answers the heartfelt prayer of faith, and He honors those who honor Him, even if they have been dishonored and ignored by people.

The God Who Hears Us

Discover the Power of Prayer

"I'd rather be able to pray than to be a great preacher; Jesus Christ
never taught his disciples how to preach, but only how to pray."

—DWIGHT L. MOODY (1837–1899)
AMERICAN BUSINESSMAN WHO BECAME A WORLD-FAMOUS EVANGELIST

MOST PEOPLE, WHETHER they are Christians or not, believe in some form of prayer—especially when they face serious problems. Even atheists may scream "God help me!" if they are in a car accident or confronted by some other sudden danger. Some people pray to stone idols, hoping their gods will give them good harvests, send rain, or kill their enemies. Some followers of New Age teachings light candles or chant spells to win favor from the invisible realm. And some people wear charms around their necks or carry certain objects in their pockets to ward off danger or invite "luck" from God.

But when Jesus came to earth He showed us that our relationship with God is not about superstition, complicated rituals, good luck, or incantations. We don't have to wear certain jewelry, recite certain magic words, or abuse our bodies to coax God into hearing us. Jesus taught that we serve a loving Father who loves us, knows our needs, and desires to bless us. He invites us to begin a relationship with Him, and then He invites us to share our needs as we talk to Him each day.

Do you want to know the secret of prayer? Do you want to see your prayers answered? The simple secret is to recognize your deep need for God. Ask yourself who you turn to first when you are in trouble. Do you spend most of your time worrying about your problems—or have you learned to trust the Lord and put your needs in His hands?

The apostle Paul gave us practical instruction about this in Philippians 4:6:

Be anxious for nothing, but in everything by prayer and supplication with thanksgiving let your requests be made known to God.

The famous Dutch evangelist Corrie ten Boom said it this way: "Dear Jesus...how foolish of me to have called for human help when You are here."[1] This is the essence of prayer—turning to God, looking to Him for help, and recognizing that He is always powerful, even though we feel powerless.

Many people assume that prayer is just a religious exercise. For example, Muslims pray five times a day, usually bowing toward Saudi Arabia as they recite a few rote prayers in Arabic. There are some Christians who attend a church service every day, and they too may recite prayers in a language they don't understand. But God doesn't require us to take a certain posture, repeat certain words, or go to a special temple or church to get His attention. He simply wants our hearts.

Some Christians have actually compared prayer to breathing. Martin Luther, the great reformer, said this: "To be a Christian without prayer is no more possible than to be alive without breathing."[2]

The Lord has given us so many promises in the Bible to remind us that He is ready to hear and answer us:

- 1 John 5:14: "This is the confidence which we have before Him, that, if we ask anything according to His will, He hears us."

- Psalm 86:7: "In the day of my trouble I shall call upon You, for You will answer me."

- Mark 11:24: "Therefore I say to you, all things for which you pray and ask, believe that you have received them, and they will be granted you."

- Psalm 17:6: "I have called upon You, for You will answer me, O God."

- Proverbs 15:29: "The LORD is far from the wicked, but He hears the prayer of the righteous."

- John 15:7: "If you abide in Me, and My words abide in you, ask whatever you wish, and it will be done for you."

Jesus was our best model for what prayer should look like. For Him prayer was not a religious exercise; it was a lifestyle of trust. He was constantly talking to the Father. After Jesus spent long days praying for the sick or demon-possessed, He would go to a lonely place to spend time in prayer. Even though He was fully God, He was fully human as well—so He needed to draw close to the Father and hear His voice.

Once you become a Christian you want to develop the habit of turning to God constantly. Another word for this is *trust*. If you trust in the Lord, you will talk to Him throughout your day about your needs, desires, worries, and challenges. You will pray for provision for your needs, wisdom for your decisions, protection from danger, healing from sickness, and strength to face each challenge. And when you trust God you know that He is not only listening to your prayers, but that He will answer.

The word *answer* appears twenty-seven times in the Book of Psalms alone. God does not tune us out or ignore us. He's listening! He is waiting for us to share our burdens and requests. He is ever ready to demonstrate His goodness. And even on our worst days we can experience answered prayer.

LET'S GO **DEEPER**

1. Read Luke 18:1–8. Jesus told a story about a woman who pestered a judge until he reluctantly gave her what she wanted. How does this parable relate to prayer?

_____

_____

_____

2. Jesus often spoke about the need for persistence in prayer. What did Jesus promise us in Matthew 7:8?

_____

_____

_____

The verbs used here in Matthew 7:8—ask, seek, and knock—are Greek present imperatives, which means they could be translated "keep on asking, keep on seeking, and keep on knocking." Prevailing prayer requires persistence.

3. Many people think prayers have to be long to be acceptable to God. But He does not require you to pray for two hours to be heard. What did Jabez pray in 1 Chronicles 4:10?

_____

_____

_____

Short prayers can be powerful. The average psalm takes only a minute or two to recite, and Psalm 117—the shortest psalm—only takes nine seconds to say. God welcomes our words, even the simplest of requests.

4. Read Romans 12:12. What should be our attitude about prayer, based on Paul's words here?

_____

We often think of the prayer of faith as triggering instant answers, but this was not always the case with Paul. While God can certainly answer immediately, He often asks us to carry a promise until we are mature enough to handle the answer.

5. How does the Holy Spirit help us in prayer, according to Romans 8:26–27?

_____

_____

_____

6. Read Matthew 18:19. What happens when two or more Christians pray together? What does it mean to "agree" in prayer?

_____

_____

_____

LET'S **TALK** ABOUT IT

Why do you think it is important for us to surrender our wills and desires to God before we pray about our own needs?

Memory Verse

Rejoice always; pray without ceasing; in everything give thanks; for this is God's will for you in Christ Jesus.

—1 THESSALONIANS 5:16–18

LET'S GO EVEN DEEPER

How Jesus Taught Us to Pray

Jesus' disciples came to Him one day and asked Him to teach them how to pray. They saw Jesus had a lifestyle of prayer, and they wanted this for themselves. Jesus gave them what we call today "The Lord's Prayer," which states:

> Our Father who is in heaven, hallowed be Your name. Your kingdom come. Your will be done, on earth as it is in heaven. Give us this day our daily bread. And forgive us our debts, as we also have forgiven our debtors. And do not lead us into temptation, but deliver us from evil. [For Yours is the kingdom and the power and the glory forever. Amen.]
>
> —MATTHEW 6:9–13

Many Christians recite this prayer every day—and there is certainly nothing wrong with doing so. But when Jesus shared this prayer with His followers He was not asking them to perform an empty ritual by simply repeating the same words over and over. Jesus was sharing from His own life how He prayed. The Lord's Prayer contains the simple components of prayer that you should also use—but you can do it in your own words, and your prayers may vary each time. Here are six key aspects of Jesus' powerful prayer:

1. Connection. Jesus prayed, "Our Father...hallowed be Your name." He looked to the true God, the Creator and Sustainer of all life. It matters who you pray to! Only when we pray to the true God can we expect to be heard.

2. Adoration. Before Jesus asked for anything He praised the one and only God. Prayer is not just asking God for things; it is worshipping Him for who He is. As you grow in prayer you will spend more time praising and thanking Him for His amazing grace.

3. Consecration. Jesus prayed, "Your kingdom come. Your will be done." In essence, He was saying, "Father, not My will but Yours be done." When we pray we should relinquish our own personal agendas and embrace God's will for our lives. Sincere prayer is not demanding God to give you what you want, but submitting to His desires for us.

4. Petition. Jesus encouraged us to pray for our daily bread. He cares about the most trivial details of our lives. He cares about our aches and pains; He cares about your lost dog, your final exam at school, or your need for a new vehicle. You are not boring Jesus with your needs. He wants to prove to you that He can provide!

5. Intercession. After we bring our own needs to God, it's a perfect time to talk to Him about others. In fact, this can be the most exciting aspect of prayer because it's so unselfish. Learn to pray about the needs of those closest to you, as well as for the needs of your community, church, nation, and world. As you grow in your relationship with God, you will learn that He wants to share His plans for the world with you, and He will invite you to pray for His will to be accomplished in certain situations.

6. Protection. Jesus also said we could pray, "Deliver us from evil." As long as we live in this broken world we should pray for God's hand to shield us from temptations and all other attacks from Satan.

HEROES OF OUR FAITH

ELISHA
The Successor of Elijah

The powerful prophet Elijah had many disciples, and he trained many schools of prophets, but no one was closer to him than his dedicated follower Elisha. After Elijah's most dramatic miracle—when he called down fire from heaven to prove God's authority over Israel—he called the young man Elisha to be trained as a prophet to take his place. From the moment Elisha sacrificed his oxen and left his father's farm he became a passionate disciple who desired to emulate his mentor.

When it was time for Elijah to end his ministry and go to heaven, Elisha displayed amazing spiritual hunger. He told his mentor that he wanted a "double portion" of the Holy Spirit's power that rested on Elijah (2 Kings 2:9). As the heavenly chariots swooped down to take Elijah to glory, the prophet threw his cloak on Elisha, signifying that God would clothe the young prophet with an even more miraculous anointing than his mentor. If you read Elisha's story in the Book of 2 Kings you learn that he performed twice as many miracles as Elijah—including the healing of a leper, the cleansing of toxic waters, and the resurrection of a dead boy.

The relationship between Elijah and Elisha is a model for us of biblical discipleship. God never intended Christians to focus all their attention on their own generation; Jesus wants us to intentionally train younger believers through mentorship and encouragement.

Living in the Supernatural

Experience the Gifts of the Holy Spirit

"Jesus gives us the gift of the Holy Spirit, yet when the Spirit comes, He
is loaded with packages! He desires to release much more in us and
through us than we could ever imagine. These gifts are given for delivery,
not for accumulation. We receive them to pass them on to others."

—JACK HAYFORD (1934–)
PENTECOSTAL AUTHOR AND PASTOR

THE BIBLE DOESN'T tell us the name of the lame beggar who sat outside the temple every day in Jerusalem. Luke tells this man's story in
Acts 3:1–10. I'm sure the poor man had a name, but to most people he was
simply "the crippled guy" they avoided when passing the gate. Maybe a
few nice folks threw coins in his cup, but most people ignored him. It is
incredibly sad that this man sat near the temple every day, but dead religion could not cure him.

But everything changed for him because of what happened on the
day of Pentecost. In that special moment, described in Acts 2:1–4, all the
disciples of Jesus who had gathered for prayer were baptized in the Holy
Spirit. They were "clothed with power," as Jesus had promised in Luke
24:49.

Now, because of that experience, Peter and John had something new.
They had seen Jesus heal paralyzed people. Because the Holy Spirit had
anointed them with supernatural power, they pulled the lame man up
on his feet, and he walked! They performed the same miracle they had
watched Jesus do several times. And the unnamed beggar began jumping
and shouting inside the temple, creating quite a stir.

This miracle must have been embarrassing for Jewish leaders since
they didn't do anything to help this man even though he had been lame
all forty years of his life. But Peter used this healing miracle to open the
door for his next sermon. He declared boldly: "It is the name of Jesus

which has strengthened this man whom you see and know" (Acts 3:16). Peter also reminded the people that this Jesus they had crucified was the Messiah, sent from God.

We don't know the specifics of the beggar's malady except that he "had been lame from his mother's womb" (v. 2) and had to be carried around. Many doctors probably tried to help him, but there was nothing they could do. Yet his dramatic healing is only the first of many miracles that were performed by the disciples in the Book of Acts. Every time a lame person walked, or a blind person's eyes were opened, or someone was delivered of a demon, the disciples probably recalled what Jesus told them while He was on earth:

> These signs will accompany those who have believed: in My name they will cast out demons, they will speak with new tongues; they will pick up serpents, and if they drink any deadly poison, it will not hurt them; they will lay hands on the sick, and they will recover.
>
> —MARK 16:17–18

Many more miracles are mentioned in the Book of Acts: a building shook during a prayer meeting in Jerusalem; paralyzed and lame people were healed in Samaria; the evangelist Philip was miraculously transported from one city to another; people were healed of diseases when Peter's shadow fell over them; Peter raised a woman named Tabitha from the dead in Lydda; Paul was directed to preach in Macedonia because of a supernatural vision; prison doors opened by themselves in Philippi; a slave girl was delivered from a demon; people were healed of different diseases in Ephesus; and a poisonous snake bit Paul on the island of Malta, yet he had no reaction to it.

These are just a few of the miracles mentioned in Acts—but we know from reading the epistles of Paul that other miraculous signs and wonders occurred when he preached in Thessalonica, Corinth, and other cities. Miracles were typical in the New Testament period. The early Christians expected miracles because Jesus had promised them. Mark's Gospel says this about the first disciples:

And they went out and preached everywhere, while the Lord worked with them, and confirmed the word by the signs that followed.

—MARK 16:20

The purpose of spiritual gifts, signs, and wonders is not to draw attention to ourselves in some sensational way. It is to "confirm" the message we preach. It is to prove that God is real and the gospel is true.

The apostle Paul explained to the Corinthians that the Holy Spirit actually gives supernatural "gifts" or "manifestations" to Christians when they receive His power. Known as *charismata* in the Greek, these gifts are the supernatural tools the early Christians used to plant churches, cast out demons, and overcome huge spiritual obstacles.

If we are full of the Spirit, we should be comfortable when the gifts of the Holy Spirit operate—whether in a church meeting, a home fellowship, or on the streets. These so-called power gifts are listed in 1 Corinthians 12:7–11, and they should be manifested regularly in any church that is open to the Spirit's work. In the passage each of these gifts are listed (emphasis added):

But to each one is given the manifestation of the Spirit for the common good. For to one is given the *word of wisdom* through the Spirit, and to another the *word of knowledge* according to the same Spirit; to another *faith* by the same Spirit, and to another *gifts of healing* by the one Spirit, and to another the *effecting of miracles*, and to another *prophecy*, and to another the *distinguishing of spirits*, to another *various kinds of tongues*, and to another the *interpretation of tongues*. But one and the same Spirit works all these things, distributing to each one individually just as He wills.

Some Christians today believe these gifts are no longer in operation, but this is because too often we lack the faith for the supernatural. Jesus certainly never told His followers that His power would stop working after one generation. The same miracles that happened in the Book of Acts are happening all over the world today. The same Spirit who worked among the first disciples wants to empower us.

LET'S GO **DEEPER**

1. Read 1 Corinthians 12:4–7. God gives different kinds of spiritual gifts. But what is the overall goal of these gifts in the church?

_____

2. Read 1 Timothy 4:14. What does the apostle Paul tell Timothy about the spiritual gifts he has been given?

_____

3. Besides the "power gifts" mentioned in 1 Corinthians 12:8–10, Paul provides another list of seven spiritual gifts in Romans 12:6–8. List them.

_____   _____

_____   _____

_____   _____

_____

4. Paul himself spoke in tongues, and he benefited from this practice. But what did he say he wanted the most, according to 1 Corinthians 14:19?

_____

_____

_____

5. Paul used his spiritual gifts, and he wanted his disciples to use spiritual gifts. But what did he say was even more important, according to 1 Corinthians 13:1–2?

_____

_____

_____

LET'S **TALK** ABOUT IT

Paul said in 1 Corinthians 14:1 that we should earnestly desire spiritual gifts. Which gifts listed in 1 Corinthians 12:7–11 would you like to have, and why?

Memory Verse

And they went out and preached everywhere, while the Lord worked with them, and confirmed the word by the signs that followed.

—MARK 16:20

LET'S GO EVEN DEEPER

We Need the Holy Spirit's Gifts Today

The apostle Paul told the Corinthians: "Pursue love, yet desire earnestly spiritual gifts" (1 Corinthians 14:1). God wants us to desire these gifts of the Holy Spirit in our lives, but He does not force us to use them. We need these nine gifts in our churches today:

1. The word of wisdom. When this gift operates, God reveals to us a supernatural solution to a problem that cannot be solved by man's good ideas. It is truly a heavenly answer.

2. The word of knowledge. The Holy Spirit sometimes reveals information that could not have been known by man. This gift was at work when Jesus looked into the Samaritan woman's heart (John 4:17–18) and knew that she had been married five times.

3. The gift of faith. This is not the normal kind of faith we need daily. The gift of faith is a special ability to believe for big things. A person operating in supernatural faith will motivate others to pray until the answer comes, or to perform a miracle.

4. The gift of healing. Paul told the Corinthians that there are actually "gifts" (plural) of healing. God is still in the business of healing bodies, minds, and broken hearts. He may want to use you to pray for physical or emotional healings for people you meet.

5. The gift of miracles. God can still open prison doors, break chains, release angelic messengers, change weather patterns, or deliver people from demons. We often hear testimonies of miracles from missionaries who are working overseas, but God can do miracles anywhere.

6. Prophecy. God loves to speak to His people, and He uses human instruments. Prophecy could be called "supernatural encouragement" because it always edifies the person who receives a word from the Lord—even if it is corrective. God may want to use you to speak a direct message to others.

7. Discernment (or "discerning of spirits"). Not all that is supernatural is from God, so we need discernment to protect us from occultism and other false spirituality. The Holy Spirit provides this gift as a way for us to tell the difference between God's work and a demonic counterfeit. We also need this gift to set people free from demons.

8. Speaking in tongues. There are "various kinds of tongues" mentioned in 1 Corinthians 12:10. Believers can have their own private prayer language, but some people are also gifted to speak in tongues in a church meeting. And there are times when Christians receive a special ability to speak in a foreign language so they can communicate the gospel.

9. Interpretation of tongues. Similar to prophecy, this gift can relay a message from God that was spoken in a foreign or angelic tongue. No language barrier can limit the Holy Spirit.

Jesus offers His miraculous power to us today so that when we preach the gospel God can confirm the message. If you want His supernatural power, ask Him for His spiritual gifts and expect them to flow.

HEROES OF OUR FAITH

BARNABAS

A Humble Encourager

The apostle Barnabas is mentioned twenty-nine times in the New Testament, but he is never actually quoted. Perhaps this is because this humble leader was so willing to serve in the background. He was a gifted preacher, but he didn't need to be in the spotlight. Originally from the island of Cyprus, Barnabas was born with the given name of Joseph, but the other apostles nicknamed him Barnabas, which means "Son of Encouragement" (Acts 4:36). The leaders in Jerusalem eventually sent him to the new, growing church in Antioch, and he "began to encourage them all with resolute heart to remain true to the Lord" (Acts 11:23). His primary motivation was to strengthen others.

Barnabas mentored the young convert named Saul—and Barnabas saw this man's potential long before others did. Saul became known as the apostle Paul, and he and Barnabas taught the new believers in Antioch and eventually traveled together, preaching in Cyprus and Asia Minor. Paul and Barnabas shared a passion to reach the Gentiles, and Paul must have learned much from his wise brother in the faith. Barnabas most certainly helped Paul formulate his views of Jesus and the gospel. Paul's profile began to increase during their years of ministry together, but Barnabas was not threatened. Always a team player, Barnabas seemed content to be in a number two position—or even last.

Some scholars believe Barnabas may have written the letter to the Hebrews in the New Testament. Others have suggested that Paul, Apollos, or even Priscilla wrote it—but no one knows for sure. If it were Barnabas, that might explain why the epistle doesn't include the author's identity in the opening salutation. Barnabas was content to be behind the scenes. He planted churches, gave generously to fund missionary work, mentored leaders, and gave his life's blood to serve the early church. We would do well to follow his example.

LESSON 23

You Are Under Construction

How God Changes Us From the Inside

*"Have thine own way, Lord! Have thine own way! Thou art
the potter, I am the clay. Mold me and make me after
thy will, while I am waiting, yielded and still."*
—ADELAIDE POLLARD GRAVE (1862–1934)
MISSIONARY AND AUTHOR OF MORE THAN ONE HUNDRED HYMNS

WHEN GOD WANTED to rebuild the city of Jerusalem, which had been destroyed by the king of Babylon, He raised up a brave leader named Nehemiah to manage the ambitious construction project. It was not an easy task. When Nehemiah did a full inspection of the damaged city he found that the walls were torn down and all the gates burned. (See Nehemiah 2:13, 17.) The city had been pillaged, and it was totally unprotected and vulnerable to invaders.

Interestingly, Nehemiah's name means "Comforter"—the same name given to the Holy Spirit in the New Testament.[1] In the Greek, "Comforter" can mean *paraclete*, or one who is "called to one's side" to help.[2] And we read in the Bible that Nehemiah led the Jews to rebuild the city brick by brick, even while their enemies were threatening to stop the work.

The ruins of Jerusalem remind us of what our lives looked like when we first came to Christ. Sin had ravaged us. Our souls were wounded and broken. We had been "burned" by our own choices and the people who hurt us. Our lives were in ruins, devastated by addiction, lust, hatred, bitterness, pride, and greed. But when the Holy Spirit moved in He began a miraculous process of transformation. This is what happens in the life of every believer in Jesus.

The Holy Spirit is the "construction manager" of this amazing but strenuous project. Like Nehemiah, He bulldozes into our lives to excavate and overhaul. He calls in His road crews, unleashes His heavy equipment, and begins what we could call an "extreme makeover." He clears out the debris, hauls off the rubbish, lays the new foundations, rehangs the doors, reconstructs the gates, and rebuilds the broken walls of our lives.

This invisible process of healing and restoration is what the Bible calls *sanctification*. This miracle is described by the apostle Paul in Titus 3:5–6:

> He saved us, not on the basis of deeds which we have done in righteousness, but according to His mercy, by the washing of regeneration and renewing by the Holy Spirit, whom He poured out upon us richly through Jesus Christ our Savior.

The Greek word used in this verse for *renewing, anakainosis*, means "a renovation or a complete change for the better."[3] Jesus loves us unconditionally, but He does not want us to stay in the same condition in which He found us. He takes us through a rigorous process of cleansing. He works on our character, our thought life, our motives, and our attitudes. He burns up the garbage of our past tendencies and removes the debris of our fears, anxieties, and resentments.

What is the Holy Spirit's ultimate goal? He wants us to become like Jesus! We see this in Romans 8:29, which says: "Those whom He foreknew, He also predestined to become conformed to the image of His Son, so that He would be the firstborn among many brethren." If we are going to become like Jesus, the Holy Spirit has much work to do. Like a sculptor, He chips away at many things in our lives that are impure, selfish, or worldly. We can't change ourselves into the image of Jesus, but the Holy Spirit can. We simply must yield to His process.

The Holy Spirit's ultimate goal is to produce Christ's character in us. The Bible calls this "the fruit of the Spirit" (Galatians 5:22). Jesus once compared Himself to a gardener, and He compared His followers to vines. Like a diligent farmer He wants to produce a bountiful crop. The process of spiritual growth is not instantaneous. No farmer grows his harvest overnight. The Spirit takes His time, and we must adjust to His schedule.

The apostle Paul told us what the Spirit is looking for in our lives. He wrote in Galatians 5:22–25:

> But the fruit of the Spirit is love, joy, peace, patience, kindness, goodness, faithfulness, gentleness, self-control; against such things there is no law. Now those who belong to Christ Jesus

have crucified the flesh with its passions and desires. If we live
by the Spirit, let us also walk by the Spirit.

German pastor Dietrich Bonhoeffer, who suffered and died in 1945
at the hands of his Nazi persecutors, noted that the fruit of the Spirit
is not something we can force or manufacture. The fruit of the Spirit
is the result of an invisible, inward process. He wrote: "Fruit is always
the miraculous, the created; it is never the result of willing, but always a
growth. The fruit of the Spirit is a gift of God, and only He can produce
it. They who bear it know as little about it as the tree knows of its fruit.
They know only the power of Him on whom their life depends."[4]

Do you want this fruit in your life? You cannot make it grow. You
cannot go to a seminar and automatically become more loving or more
patient. It is impossible for a human being to conform himself to the
character of Jesus; instead we must yield to the Spirit and let Him change
us. He wants to bring all nine of these qualities into our lives:

1. Love. If you want more love, that means the Holy Spirit must deal
with your selfishness, anger, and resentment.

2. Joy. What if you prayed for more joy? God will have to remove your
tendency to whine and complain.

3. Peace. If the Holy Spirit brings His peace, you will have to give Him
your anxieties and fears.

4. Patience. If you want more patience, you will have to learn to rest
in God's timing and embrace delays.

5. Kindness. Will you learn to show forgiveness and compassion to
people who don't deserve to be treated with kindness? The Holy Spirit
teaches us how to do this.

6. Goodness. What if you prayed that God would make you more
generous? Are you willing to surrender your wallet to Him? The Holy
Spirit will cut to the root of any greed in your life.

7. Faithfulness. Even if you have been an erratic and unstable person
in the past, God can make you consistent and trustworthy.

8. Gentleness. The Holy Spirit may put His finger on your anger and
dig up some deep hurts that have caused you to be harsh to others. Jesus
can make you tender and loving.

9. Self-control. Are you willing to ask the Holy Spirit to break any
harmful addictions that have enslaved you? Regardless of what controlled you in the past, sin does not have to rule your life.

Philippians 1:6 reminds us that it is God, not us, who engineers our personal transformation:

> For I am confident of this very thing, that He who began a good
> work in you will perfect it until the day of Christ Jesus.

Remember, you cannot grow the fruit of the Spirit yourself. That is not your job. You must invite the indwelling Spirit to work in you. Let Him change you. Let Jesus pull out all His tools so He can carefully dig, chop, cut, water, fertilize, and prune you until He produces a harvest that brings Him joy.

LET'S GO **DEEPER**

1. According to 2 Corinthians 3:18, we are being transformed as we behold God's glory. Who is responsible for this miraculous transformation?

_____

_____

2. Ephesians 4:24 says we should "put on the new self" as if we were putting on new clothes. What does this new self look like?

_____

_____

_____

3. Read the ancient prophecy of Malachi in Malachi 3:2–3. Jesus is compared to fire and soap in this passage, and then He is compared to a man who heats up silver and melts it to remove the impurities from the metal. What does God say will happen to His followers after this process?

_____

_____

4. Read Romans 12:1-2. Paul tells us not to conform to the world but to be "transformed" by the renewing of our minds. What will we learn if we do this?

_____

_____

_____

According to this passage in Romans, inner transformation comes as we submit ourselves to God. For centuries Christians have called this the act of *consecration*—which means "to devote irrevocably to the worship of God by a solemn ceremony."[5] When we bow our hearts to God in full surrender and say, "Lord, have Your way in me," we allow the Holy Spirit to change us. Full surrender removes all obstacles so that God can change our attitudes, bend our wills, purify our motives, reorder our priorities, crush our sinful habits, and make us more like Jesus. Don't just consecrate your life to God occasionally. Jesus calls us to a life of continual consecration.

LET'S **TALK** ABOUT IT

Look back at the list of the different fruit of the Holy Spirit. Which one of these qualities do you need the most, and why?

Memory Verse

Therefore if anyone is in Christ, he is a new creature; the old things passed away; behold, new things have come.
—2 Corinthians 5:17

LET'S GO EVEN DEEPER
Let Jesus Change You Daily

So many of us struggle with a damaged self-image. We want to believe God loves us, but our negative experiences have programmed us to reject the truth. Maybe this has been your experience. You want to believe the Bible, but on most days you think you are a failure, stupid, weak, inferior, disqualified, or unlovable.

How can you stop these wrong patterns of thinking? You must listen to what God says about you. Romans 12:2 says: "Be transformed by the renewing of your mind." There are so many scriptures that describe your true identity. Meditate on the following Bible verses so you can overcome the lies you have believed about yourself. Speak these words regularly and let them heal your self-image:

I am loved. Jeremiah 31:3 says: "I have loved you with an everlasting love; I have drawn you with unfailing kindness." God's love for me is so great it is difficult to fathom. It will take all of eternity to fully comprehend how great His love is. In spite of my mistakes, my weaknesses, and my sins, God is kind and merciful, and He loves me unconditionally.

I am a child of God. My Father delights in me as a son or daughter. He is not angry with me. My loving Father accepts me and celebrates me. Ephesians 1:6 says, "He made us accepted in the Beloved" (NKJV). I am welcome in my Father's house!

I am forgiven. I have been washed in the blood of Christ. I am clean. He does not keep a file on my sins. He has purged everything from my record. He even chose to forget my sins. Ephesians 1:7 says, "We have redemption through His blood, the forgiveness of sins, according to the riches of His grace" (NKJV).

I am blameless. When God looks at me, He sees the righteousness of Jesus, not my sin. He took my filthy garments and gave me a new robe of righteousness. Ephesians 1:4 says He chose us before the foundation of the world, "that we would be holy and blameless before Him."

I have been adopted. The Father wanted me in His family. He paid the ultimate price so I could be His child. He drew me from far away so I could live with Him forever. I belong to Him! Romans 8:15 says I have "received the spirit of adoption by whom we cry out, 'Abba, Father'" (NKJV). I can call God my Daddy!

I am an heir with Christ. I have a spiritual inheritance. Everything that belongs to the Father has been given to me. God does not withhold His goodness from me. Romans 8:17 says I am an "heir of God" and a "fellow heir with Christ." Ephesians 1:3 says we have been blessed with every spiritual blessing in Christ.

I am free from sin. Sin doesn't have power over me. I can flee from temptation. Romans 6:18 says I am now a "slave of righteousness" because I've been freed from my past sins and addictions. Second Corinthians 5:17 says if anyone is in Christ, the old things have passed away and "all things have become new."

I am victorious. I am not just a conqueror. Romans 8:37 says I am more than a conqueror because of Him who loved us (NKJV). Because of the victory Christ won on the cross for me, I have also overcome sin and death. First John 4:4 says, "Greater is He who is in you than He who is in the world." The devil has been defeated!

I am the temple of the Holy Spirit. God's Holy Spirit lives in me, according to 1 Corinthians 6:19. I am never alone. God's presence is always with me because His Holy Spirit abides in me forever. And Jesus promised He will never leave me nor forsake me. He will never take His Holy Spirit from me.

I have received power. I've been filled with the Holy Spirit. Now I can lay hands on the sick and see them healed. I can cast out demons. I have authority over all the devil's power. Jesus said in Luke 10:19: "I have given you authority to tread on serpents and scorpions, and over all the power of the enemy."

I am a spiritual warrior. I wear the armor of God. I have the shield of faith, the helmet of salvation, and the sword of the Spirit. The devil will not be able to defeat me. Ephesians 6:10 says I am strong in the Lord and in the strength of His might. Even when I feel weak I am strong because the Holy Spirit empowers me.

I have the peace of God. I will not be shaken by worry, fear, or anxiety. God comforts me and calms my fears. Philippians 4:7 says the peace of God, which surpasses all comprehension, will guard my heart and mind in Christ Jesus. I am not controlled by fear. Psalm 118:6 says: "The LORD is for me; I will not fear."

I am guided by God's Spirit. The Lord is my Shepherd, and He leads me and guides me. I can hear His still, gentle voice. Psalm 32:8 promises me: "I will instruct you and teach you in the way which you should go." God directs my steps, gives me wisdom, and helps me make the right choices.

I am full of God's joy. My joy is not based on my circumstances. I can rejoice no matter what is going on in my life. When I feel discouraged, Nehemiah 8:10 promises: "The joy of the LORD is your strength." Even when I go through hard times I know the pain will not last forever. I have the promise of Psalm 30:5: "Weeping may last for the night, but a shout of joy comes in the morning."

I am an ambassador for Christ. I can reconcile others to Jesus Christ. Everywhere I go people will be drawn to Jesus. Second Corinthians 5:20 says God has made me an ambassador. And 2 Corinthians 3:6 says God has made me an adequate minister of the new covenant. I am qualified, not because of my own abilities but because God has qualified me.

I am God's masterpiece. God created me for a special purpose. He will use me to do good works that will bring glory to the Father. Ephesians 2:10 says I am God's "workmanship"—which means "masterpiece." I am on a divine assignment, and I will fulfill God's mission for my life!

I am blessed. God sees me and cares for me. He is a good Father. He provides for my daily needs. Luke 6:38 says when I give to others, God will give to me "pressed down, shaken together, running over." I will experience His supernatural provision. And Philippians 4:19 says, "My God supplies all of my need according to His riches in glory by Christ Jesus."

I am growing as a disciple. I am growing more stable every day because Jesus is my foundation. When I feel weak, confused, unstable, or tormented, I will find peace and stability in Christ, who is my refuge. Colossians 2:7 says I am "firmly rooted and now being built up in Him and established in [my] faith." Because I have strong roots in Christ, I will bear much fruit for God.

I always have access to His grace. Jesus has given me strength for every trial I face. He promises me in 2 Corinthians 12:9: "My grace is sufficient for you, for power is perfected in weakness." There will always be enough strength to face each day, no matter how weak I feel. God's grace will never run out.

I will live forever with Christ. Romans 6:23 says, "The free gift of God is eternal life in Christ Jesus our Lord." I will spend eternity in the presence of God. Revelation 21:27 says my name has been written in the Lamb's Book of Life; therefore I will dwell in the heavenly city with Christ when this life is over.

Declare these truths over your life regularly. Let the Word of God transform the way you see yourself.

HEROES OF OUR FAITH

JUDE

He Stood for Truth

Like his brother James, Jude was from the family of Joseph and Mary, so he grew up knowing Jesus as a brother. But he didn't follow Him during His earthly ministry. Jude came to believe that Jesus was the Son of God after the resurrection, but that didn't disqualify him from having a powerful ministry in the first century. He wrote a short letter in the New Testament—one of the five shortest books—yet the founders of the early church agreed that his letter was inspired by the Holy Spirit.

While Jude did not recognize Jesus' deity when he was young, his epistle emphatically states this truth. He refers to Jesus as "Lord" multiple times (Jude 1:4, 17, 21, 25), reminding us that Jesus is our ultimate authority. The focus of Jude's strongly worded letter was to warn Christians of dangerous false teachers who claimed to carry the gospel message when they were actually imposters. Jude said these deceivers, like wolves, had "crept in unnoticed" so they could "turn the grace of our God into licentiousness and deny our only Master and Lord, Jesus Christ" (v. 4). He warned that people would claim to be preachers of the gospel, and yet they would practice sexual immorality and all forms of moral and financial corruption.

Jude's short but powerful message, found near the end of the Bible, reminds us that Satan will do everything he can to deceive Christians, distort the truth, and divide the church. He challenges all followers of Jesus to "contend earnestly for the faith which was once for all handed down to the saints" (v. 3). This is why you must grow strong, not only in the knowledge of the Word of God, but in godly character. May we all be like Jude, who did not compromise the gospel message!

Digging for Divine Truth

How to Study the Bible

"The Bible is no lazy man's book! Much of its treasure, like
the valuable minerals stored in the bowels of the earth,
only yield up themselves to the diligent seeker."

—ARTHUR PINK (1886–1952)
AUTHOR AND THEOLOGIAN

BACK IN THE days of Jesus, people didn't have their own copies of the Scriptures. Scribes carefully made copies of the Old Testament onto papyrus scrolls or animal skins, which were then kept in synagogues and viewed only by rabbis. Many common people, and almost all women, were illiterate. The Jews would listen to a rabbi read from the Scriptures, and this was their only opportunity to hear God's Word. The ordinary Jew didn't have an Old Testament on his bookshelf or by his bedside table.

After the church began to grow, copies of different parts of the New Testament circulated among the congregations. Church leaders met to discern which writings were inspired by the Holy Spirit, and these were eventually "canonized," or recognized as official. The first actual copy of the New Testament, on a scroll, did not appear until sometime around AD 175. Until then Christians only heard the Scriptures read aloud to them.

What we call "books" today didn't appear until around AD 320. Then in AD 405 a man named Jerome finished translating the New Testament into Latin (it took him twenty-three years), but copies of this Latin Vulgate Bible were circulated only among church leaders. By AD 600 the New Testament had been translated into eight languages.

During the Middle Ages monks were viewed as the guardians of the Bible, and they spent their lives making meticulous, handwritten copies of the Scriptures. But these copies were very expensive, so they were kept only in churches or monasteries. In fact, priests taught that ordinary people should not study the Bible since they would not understand it!

Then in 1229 a church council ruled that only priests could own a copy of the Bible. This ruling led some people to illegally distribute contraband Bibles. Finally, a brave scholar named John Wycliffe made the first English translation of the Bible in 1382. He declared: "Every Christian ought to study this book because it is the whole truth."[1] Wycliffe got into serious trouble with the Catholic Church because he taught that the Scriptures, not the pope, were God's ultimate authority.

After Wycliffe died from a stroke in 1384, church officials declared anyone who translated the Bible into the language of the common people guilty of heresy. Church leaders even exhumed Wycliffe's body and burned it to send a strong message that they would not tolerate such "crimes" as Bible translation. So the English Bible went underground for 130 years.

But the spread of the gospel could not be stopped. The biggest breakthrough came in 1455, when a German inventor named Johannes Gutenberg printed the Bible on the first moveable-type printing press. This machine made books available to common people, sparked a rise in literacy, advanced scientific discovery, and spread Christianity far and wide. Even though Gutenberg was not a successful businessman and died in relative obscurity, today he is recognized as one of the world's most influential people because his printing press changed history forever.

Today the full Bible has been translated into 717 languages and the New Testament into another 1,582 languages.[2] Thanks to digital technology, Bible stories and biblical teachings are available to billions of people through videos, movies, cartoons, recorded sermons, and digitized Scripture. Never has the Bible been more accessible.

Yet despite the enormous price so many people paid for us to access the Bible, we often neglect it. If you want to go deeper in your relationship with God, develop the habit of reading and studying His Word. If you fall in love with the Bible and value it for the precious treasure that it is, God will speak to you from its pages regularly and strengthen you with its truth.

LET'S GO **DEEPER**

1. What did the apostle Paul say about God's Word in 2 Timothy 2:9?

This verse helps us understand why the Bible's influence has continued to multiply over the centuries. No matter what powers have tried to get rid of the Bible, its message keeps spreading.

2. What did Paul tell Timothy to do in his congregation while he was waiting for Paul to return, according to 1 Timothy 4:13?

_____

_____

3. Ezra loved God and led the Jewish people during a difficult period in Israel's history. What did Ezra do with the Scriptures, according to Ezra 7:10?

_____

_____

4. Read Proverbs 4:10–13. What will happen if we accept the Bible's sayings?

_____

_____

_____

LET'S **TALK** ABOUT IT

Tell about a time when the Holy Spirit spoke to you while you were studying the Bible. What did He show you?

Memory Verse

I will meditate on Your precepts and regard Your ways. I shall delight in Your statutes; I shall not forget Your word.

—Psalm 119:15–16

LET'S GO EVEN DEEPER

Practical Tips for Bible Study

Many Christians are too busy to spend some quiet time with God. But you will not grow spiritually if you don't develop a habit of personal time in prayer and Bible reading. Here are some ways you can make your time in God's Word richer and more intimate:

Set a regular time for your "date" with God. There's no rule about when to pray and study. Some people prefer mornings; others find prayer easier in the evening hours. Once you develop your unique habit, and you realize how much you benefit from it, you'll find you simply can't live without your devotional time.

Choose a special place that gives you privacy. Jesus reminded us that seclusion is a secret to meaningful devotion. He said: "But you, when you pray, enter your closet, and when you have shut your door, pray to your Father who is in secret" (Matthew 6:6, mev). You need a quiet place to read and study so you can focus. And don't forget to silence your phone!

Don't put yourself under pressure. You don't have to read fifty chapters of the Bible in one sitting. Pace yourself. Be realistic and take small steps. Start by reading a chapter a day in the Bible and praying for fifteen minutes. Eventually you will want more. The key is to be consistent.

Use a study Bible. You wouldn't understand a Shakespearean play if you read the original manuscript from 1595. The English language has changed a lot since then. The only way to understand a Shakespearean play is to read an annotated version that explains difficult words and passages. In the same way, study Bibles provide helpful footnotes.

Choose a readable translation. Modern translations, such as the New International Version or the New American Standard Bible, are easier to read. Keep other translations handy, including the Amplified Version, to compare verses. You can use an online Bible like the YouVersion to read different translations at once.

Learn to "chew" the Bible. One of the simplest ways to study the Bible is to read one book at a time (such as Romans or Isaiah) and slowly digest each verse, chapter by chapter. Studying the Bible is sometimes compared to a cow chewing its cud over and over. The more you read a passage, the more "juice" you squeeze out of it!

Listen for God's voice. God wants to speak directly to you through the pages of His Word. When you read Scripture with a prayerful heart, God can cause a verse to jump off the page as a direct, personal message. British preacher Charles Spurgeon wrote: "When I have been in trouble, I have read the Bible until a text has seemed to stand out of the Book, and salute me, saying, 'I was written specially for you.'"[3]

Use study helps. *Strong's Exhaustive Concordance of the Bible* allows you to look up any word in the Old Testament Hebrew or the New Testament Greek. You can find out the original meaning of the word, providing deeper insight. This tool, as well as *Matthew Henry's Commentary on the Whole Bible,* are both available online.

Expect to gain revelation. Before you read the Bible, ask the Holy Spirit to shine His light on your mind and reveal truth to you. Ask the Lord to give you insights into His Word. Proverbs 2:2, 4–5 says, "Make your ear attentive to wisdom, incline your heart to understanding...if you seek her as silver and search for her as hidden treasures; then you will discern the fear of the LORD and discover the knowledge of God." It is important to come to the Word with a seeking heart.

Write down your insights. Keep a notebook or your iPad nearby so you can record what God shows you. You can also record revelations you receive by writing them in the margins of your Bible. Writing these down will help you remember them.

Apply the Word to your life. Because the Bible is a divinely inspired book, it always offers relevant application to life situations. Ask questions after you read: "What does this passage tell me about the character of God?" "What does it tell me about Jesus Christ?" "What other truths does it reveal?" "What does this passage tell me to do, and how can I respond in obedience?"

Become a gold miner. Studying the Bible is like mining for precious metals or jewels. Expect to find treasure! When you read the Book of Acts, for example, you can look for references to the Holy Spirit's supernatural power and find much revelation. But then when you read it a second time, look for references to crossing racial and ethnic boundaries. A third time you can read it from the angle of prayer. Every book of the Bible is like a multifaceted diamond, and light will sparkle from every angle.

HEROES OF OUR FAITH

JOB

He Endured Suffering

Job is the oldest book in the Bible. A wealthy landowner with ten children, Job was a righteous, God-fearing man from the land of Uz—which was probably in modern Saudi Arabia. Scholars are not sure who wrote his story, yet Job's testimony of perseverance in the midst of suffering still brings great comfort to people all over the world today.

Satan wanted to prove to God that Job would not serve Him if he experienced hardship. So Job experienced a series of painful calamities including sickness, loss of property, and the deaths of his children. None of this seems fair, yet the Book of Job offers a profound look at the issue of suffering and why God allows it. In the end we learn that Job did not suffer because of his own sin but simply because sometimes God allows tests and trials in our lives for His own purposes. God wanted Job to understand that even when bad things happen to good people, He is still God and we are not.

At the conclusion of Job's trials everything he lost was restored double, and he even had ten more children. Job's story is painful to read, but the final outcome is summarized in Job 42:10: "The LORD restored the fortunes of Job." During Job's journey toward spiritual growth he also had a profound revelation of the coming Messiah. Job said: "As for me, I know that my Redeemer lives, and at the last He will take His stand on the earth." It is amazing that this ancient Bible character, who probably lived before Abraham, received a prophecy about the coming of Jesus Christ. Since the beginning of history God has always planned to send Jesus to redeem us.

Our Wilderness Journey

Staying Strong During Tests and Trials

"When we long for life without difficulties, remind us that oaks grow
strong in contrary winds and diamonds are made under pressure."

—PETER MARSHALL (1902–1949)
AMERICAN PREACHER WHO SERVED AS CHAPLAIN OF THE US SENATE

WHEN WE BEGIN our journey with Jesus we learn that He has many
wonderful blessings in store for us: salvation from sin, the promise
of eternal life, freedom from guilt, the blessings of answered prayer, and
so many other benefits. But this doesn't mean Christians don't have
problems. We live in a broken world overrun with sin, and that means as
long as we are on this side of eternity we will have struggles.

There are Christian preachers today who claim that all our difficulties
disappear when we begin following the Lord. They say if you have
enough faith you will never get sick, never have an accident, and never
face financial problems. Some preachers will even try to convince you
that if you quote a Bible verse long enough, or pray hard enough, or give
plenty of money in offerings, God will bless you with unlimited success,
health, and wealth. Some people have nicknamed these people "prosperity
preachers" because they insist that faith in Jesus will guarantee you a
problem-free, stress-free life of ease.

Where did we ever get the idea that following Jesus would be easy?
Jesus told His disciples: "You will be hated by all because of My name"
(Mark 13:13). Paul told Timothy: "Indeed, all who desire to live godly in
Christ Jesus will be persecuted" (2 Timothy 3:12). Never forget there is a
cost to serving God.

People who followed God in the Bible suffered in many ways. The
ancient Job, whose story is one of the oldest in the Bible, lost everything
he had, including his family. Sarah struggled with years of infertility.
Joseph's own brothers sold him into slavery. Naomi became a widow and

lost her two sons. David had to hide for his life for years while King Saul hunted him down like an animal. In the New Testament, most of Jesus' disciples were persecuted and killed for preaching the gospel. And the apostle Paul was beaten with rods, stoned, and left for dead by an angry mob, betrayed by friends, shipwrecked, and imprisoned for his faith.

Yet Paul did not allow his problems to shake his faith. Once when Roman officials imprisoned him, Paul wrote the short letter to the Philippians, which is sometimes called "the epistle of joy" because it contains the words *joy* or *rejoicing* sixteen times. In the letter's four short chapters Paul continually exhorts us to praise God no matter how dark our circumstances are. He writes: "I will rejoice" (Philippians 1:18), "I rejoice and share my joy with you all" (2:17), "I urge you, rejoice in the same way" (2:18), "Finally, my brethren, rejoice in the Lord" (3:1), and "Rejoice in the Lord always; again I will say, rejoice!" (4:4).

After telling his friends in Philippi how much he loved them, and that he was praying for them while in prison, he said:

> Now I want you to know, brethren, that my circumstances have turned out for the greater progress of the gospel, so that my imprisonment in the cause of Christ has become well known throughout the whole praetorian guard and to everyone else, and that most of the brethren, trusting in the Lord because of my imprisonment, have far more courage to speak the word of God without fear.
>
> —PHILIPPIANS 1:12–14

Can you hear Paul's enthusiasm? He has every reason to complain—about his chains, the meager food rations, and the mistreatment by Roman soldiers. But Paul was actually thankful in the midst of his difficult circumstances because He saw God's hand at work. Even though he was uncomfortable, and his freedoms had been taken from him, he found something good in the middle of his trial. This is why he could say: "Rejoice in the Lord always." Whenever you read those words remember that they were written by a man in chains.

In another of Paul's letters he talked about the way God uses our trials and difficult moments to shape our character and spiritual fruitfulness. He told the Corinthians: "For momentary, light affliction is producing for us an eternal weight of glory far beyond all comparison" (2 Corinthians

4:17). If we understand this deep truth we will respond differently when we face life's challenges. Instead of whining and complaining like selfish babies we will step back, recognize that God is with us in the trial, and rejoice that He will walk with us through the challenge.

We see this process in the life of David. During his long journey to becoming king, David ended up in an obscure town called Ziklag. Scholars aren't sure where this place was, only that it was in the remote Judean wilderness. Ziklag means "pressure," and it refers to the process of shaping molten metal. While David was in this dark place he wrote, "My soul thirsts for You...in a dry and weary land where there is no water" (Psalm 63:1).

David didn't lose faith while he was suffering. He stayed thirsty for God. He prayed constantly—knowing that he was in the fire of testing. God was applying heat and pressure to shape him for greater responsibility. In the end David got out of Ziklag and sat on the throne in Jerusalem. What was David's secret to enduring trials? Like Paul, David obviously knew how to rejoice when he didn't feel like it. After all, David wrote most of the psalms—which are songs he wrote when he faced unimaginable problems.

Way back in 1970 a military chaplain named Merlin Carothers wrote a small book called *Prison to Praise*. Today it has sold more than seventeen million copies in fifty-three languages. It challenges readers to thank and praise God in the midst of difficulties—and it's full of testimonies of everyday people who experienced miraculous breakthroughs when they obeyed this simple principle.

What Carothers wrote more than fifty years ago is still relevant today: "The very act of praise releases the power of God into a set of circumstances and enables God to change them. Miracles, power and victory will all be a part of what God does in our lives when we learn to rejoice in all things."[1]

LET'S GO **DEEPER**

1. Read 1 Peter 4:12–13. How should we respond when we experience trials, difficulties, or suffering of any kind?

_____

_____

_____

2. Read 1 Peter 5:10. What does Peter say will happen to us after we have suffered for a little while?

_____

_____

_____

3. According to Romans 5:3–4, what do our sufferings eventually produce?

_____

_____

_____

4. Read Psalm 27:5–6. What will God do for us in the day of trouble?

_____

_____

_____

5. In this psalm, in verse 6, what did David do when he faced difficulties?

_____

_____

6. Read 1 Peter 4:19. What should we do when we suffer in any way?

_____

_____

_____

7. According to James 1:2–3, what should be our attitude when we experience different kinds of trials? And what do these trials produce in our lives?

_____

_____

_____

LET'S **TALK** ABOUT IT

What's the most difficult trial you've endured recently? Be honest: Were you able to rejoice in the midst of it?

Memory Verse

For I consider that the sufferings of this present time are not worthy to be compared with the glory that is to be revealed to us.
—ROMANS 8:18

HEROES OF OUR FAITH

PHILIP

He Witnessed the Holy Spirit's Power

The first Christians were all Jews, but quickly the Holy Spirit began to dismantle racial and ethnic walls. The Book of Acts tells us that the apostles chose some Greeks to serve as leaders in the church—and one of them was a man named Philip. His Greek name tells us that he came from a non-Israelite family. In Acts 8 he traveled to Samaria—a place that Jews avoided—and boldly preached the gospel there to people who were from a different racial background. Many sick people were healed, and others were delivered from demons.

On Philip's journey back to Jerusalem, an angel directed him to witness to an influential Ethiopian man who was traveling on a desert road. This man was most likely a convert to Judaism, but after listening to Philip's teaching he declared: "I believe that Jesus Christ is the Son of God" (Acts 8:37). He wanted to be baptized immediately, so Philip fulfilled that request. Then the Spirit "snatched Philip away" (v. 39) to an area on the Mediterranean Sea, where he preached in other cities until he stopped in Caesarea, the capital of Roman Judea. Philip made that city his ministry base as he continued to proclaim the gospel.

In Philip's life we see the passion that burned in the hearts of early Christians. They were willing to cross deserts, mountain ranges, and oceans to take the message of Jesus to all nations. Philip was willing to preach to Samaritans, whom Jews considered outcasts. He also went out of his way to talk to the Ethiopian, and history tells us that this convert returned to his homeland to plant the first Christian church in Ethiopia. Philip shows us how God desires to use each one of us to extend Christ's kingdom to new people and places until everyone has heard. We all need Philip's courage!

LESSON 26

God's Global Mission

Why We Must Spread the Gospel

"If I had a thousand lives, China should have them."
—J. Hudson Taylor (1832–1905)
British Missionary to China

WHEN HE WAS on earth, Jesus spent almost all His time in the tiny land of Israel, which may have had a population of five hundred thousand people. Jesus ventured outside the borders of Palestine only a few times. He spoke to some crowds, and many in Israel heard about Him because of His miracles and teachings, but He focused most of His attention on a small number of disciples. And when He died and was resurrected, He initially had only a few hundred followers.

But Jesus had an ambitious goal that went far beyond the borders of Palestine, which was about the size of New Jersey. He didn't go to all the trouble of coming to earth, living a sinless life, and being crucified on a Roman cross just so He could touch a small number of people. Even though He lived humbly, in an obscure corner of the globe, He told His followers that His mission was bigger than they could dream.

- Jesus said in John 12:47: "I did not come to judge the world, but to save the world."
- The apostle John said that Jesus was sent to be "the Savior of the world" (1 John 4:14).
- Jesus told His disciples after His resurrection that He wanted them to go everywhere. He said: "Go into all the world and preach the gospel to all creation" (Mark 16:15).

All the world? Yes, this was always Jesus' grand plan. He knew He would die on a cruel cross in a tiny Roman outpost in the Middle East, but He commanded His disciples to take the good news of salvation everywhere. In the first century the world's population was only two hundred million people—much less than the population of the United States today.[1] Jesus knew that the world would soon have billions of people, yet He commissioned His disciples to take His message to every village, every tribe, every city regardless of size, and every country.

Jesus often spoke to His disciples using agricultural imagery because everyone in those times understood farming. He compared the work of spreading the gospel to planting and harvesting crops, and He compared Christians to the "laborers" who did the work. In one of His most famous parables, or stories, He spoke about a farmer who sowed seed in four different types of soil: (1) beside a road where birds gobbled up the seeds, (2) on rocky ground where it was difficult to grow crops, (3) in thorny fields where healthy crops could not flourish, and (4) on good soil where it was easy for plants to grow and produce fruits, vegetables, or grains. (See Mark 4:3–8.)

Jesus then explained to His followers that the farmer represented the person who shares the message of God's Word to others. He was preparing them for their mission. Jesus gave another agricultural parable in Mark 4:30–32, again involving a seed. He said:

> The kingdom of God...is like a mustard seed, which, when sown upon the soil, though it is smaller than all the seeds that are upon the soil, yet when it is sown, it grows up and becomes larger than all the garden plants and forms large branches; so that the birds of the air can nest under its shade.

Have you ever seen a mustard seed? It is a tiny black speck, as small as a grain of sand. And yet from that tiny seed, a large plant grows that produces a crop. Jesus told this story to prepare His followers, and us, for the miracle that would happen after He died for us. Jesus was predicting that His message would go viral and that the church would spread to every part of the globe.

After Jesus was raised from the dead, He gave His disciples what we now call the Great Commission. He sent them out from Israel to preach the message of salvation in Christ. Just before He ascended into heaven, He stood on a mountain east of Jerusalem and said:

> But you will receive power when the Holy Spirit has come upon
> you; and you shall be My witnesses both in Jerusalem, and in all
> Judea and Samaria, and even to the remotest part of the earth.
>
> —Acts 1:8

In the Book of Acts, we have a carefully researched history of the first few decades of the early Christian movement. The first disciples, filled with the Holy Spirit's zeal and courage, preached to Jews in Jerusalem, then spread to other parts of their country and began discipling Italians and other foreigners. They quickly spread the gospel to what is now Turkey, then to Greece, and then to Rome.

In the letters of Paul we find that he was planning a trip to Spain (Romans 15:28) and that his disciple Titus had left the island of Crete to plant a church in Dalmatia, which is modern Croatia. We also know from historic records that some of Jesus' other disciples took the gospel to Egypt, Libya, Persia, India, and other parts of Europe—all in just one generation. The tiny mustard seed Jesus planted grew rapidly.

Fast-forward to today, and you will find 2.6 billion people who claim to be Christians around the world—including many believers who suffer for their faith in nations such as North Korea, Saudi Arabia, Cuba, Uzbekistan, China, and Iran.[2] The mustard tree has grown huge, but there are still many people who have never heard the gospel one time.

Jesus is waiting for us to finish the job He gave us. But what will motivate us to accomplish this task? Just before Jesus sent His disciples out to preach for the first time, He observed the crowds who were following Him. He saw the pain in their faces; He felt sadness when He noticed their physical ailments. Matthew 9:36–38 says:

> Seeing the people, He felt compassion for them, because they
> were distressed and dispirited like sheep without a shepherd.
> Then He said to His disciples, "The harvest is plentiful, but the
> workers are few. Therefore beseech the Lord of the harvest to
> send out workers into His harvest."

Do you love lost people enough to share Jesus with them? In the 1800s British pastor Charles Spurgeon called his converts to care about the lost. He said: "If sinners will be damned, at least let them leap to hell over our bodies; and if they will perish, let them perish with our arms about their knees, imploring them to stay, and not madly to destroy themselves. If hell must be filled, at least let it be filled in the teeth of our exertions, and let not one go there unwarned and unprayed for."[3]

The Lord's global mission is our mission. Each of us is called to share our faith, make disciples, and work to spread His love and compassion. What will motivate us to do this? We must have the same compassion Jesus felt when He observed the multitudes. If we love people as He loves them, we will be willing to do whatever it requires to take God's message of love and forgiveness to them.

LET'S GO **DEEPER**

1. Read 2 Peter 3:9. What does God desire for all people?

_____

2. The early Christians in the Book of Acts did not let fear stop them from sharing their faith. What happened in Acts 4:31 when they were filled with the Holy Spirit?

_____

_____

_____

3. Read the last two verses in the Book of Acts, which are Acts 28:30–31. What do we see Paul doing in this last scene?

_____

_____

_____

4. Read Romans 1:16. What should be our attitude regarding talking to others about Jesus and salvation?

_____

5. Read 2 Corinthians 5:20. How does the apostle Paul describe our job, and what are we supposed to say when we talk to unbelievers about Jesus Christ?

_____

_____

_____

6. Read 2 Timothy 1:7–8. The apostle Paul has some sobering instructions to his spiritual son Timothy, urging him to preach the gospel without fear. If we are going to finish the task of world evangelism, what will it require of us?

_____

_____

_____

LET'S **TALK** ABOUT IT

Describe your biggest fear when it comes to talking to others about Jesus.

Memory Verse

For I am not ashamed of the gospel, for it is the power of God for salvation to everyone who believes, to the Jew first and also to the Greek.

—ROMANS 1:16

LET'S GO EVEN DEEPER

Prepare Your Heart to Go

When you read the Book of Acts you'll discover that almost all the ministry of the early church took place outside of Christian meetings. Of course, the first disciples met together for encouragement, teaching, and fellowship, but their primary focus was always outreach to people who did not know Jesus.

Christianity is always focused outward, not inward. This should also be our pattern. Our hearts should always be ready to "go"—whether our mission is to go and preach in a foreign country or to share Jesus with our next-door neighbors. If you want to be focused on the harvest Jesus calls us to reach, do the following.

Ask for the Holy Spirit's power. The first outreach in the Book of Acts occurred immediately after the disciples were filled with the Holy Spirit. The apostle Peter, who had denied Jesus just weeks before, boldly preached in a public place—and three thousand people were converted (Acts 2:41). You may feel fearful about sharing your faith, but you will receive supernatural confidence to speak when you are baptized in the Holy Spirit. Lack of emphasis on the Spirit's power is the main reason Christians are timid when it comes to evangelism.

Look for opportunities. Peter and John were on their way to the temple to worship when they saw a lame man who needed healing (Acts 3:1–3). They prayed for him, and the subsequent miracle led to more conversions. Your biggest opportunity may be on the street corner outside the church. Tune your ear to the open doors around you.

Almost all ministry encounters in the Book of Acts took place outside of religious buildings. Many of the people we are called to reach will never go near our churches. We must take Christ to the marketplace through home churches, workplace Bible studies, campus ministries, street meetings—and into cyberspace by using online platforms.

Expect miracles. In the early church miracles of healing took place in the streets after they preached (Acts 5:14–16). You don't have to be a theologian to share the gospel—just offer to pray for someone, and see what happens! God wants to use you to heal the sick, comfort the depressed, set free the addicted, or provide food for a person who is struggling financially.

Be willing to go to out-of-the-way places. God told the evangelist Philip to leave the exciting revival meetings in Samaria and go to a remote place on a desert road (Acts 8:26). His obedience led to the conversion of the Ethiopian eunuch, who then planted the gospel in that nation. Never downplay the importance of one-on-one conversations. God's biggest surprises are often found on desert roads, and sometimes the most strategic ministry moments involve just one spiritually desperate individual.

Be willing to cross cultural barriers. Peter didn't want to go to the house of Cornelius because Jews didn't visit the homes of Italians. But when he followed the Holy Spirit's leading and walked into that house full of foreigners, the gospel jumped over the cultural firewall and a new subculture was introduced to Jesus (Acts 10:44–45). As you pray about where to do outreach, don't allow racial barriers to limit you.

Pray for compassion. You will not talk to people about their need for salvation if you don't care about them. David Brainerd was a young missionary who gave his life to reach Native Americans in the colonies in the 1700s. He wrote: "I care not where I go, or how I live, or what I endure so that I may save souls. When I sleep I dream of them; when I awake they are first in my thoughts."[4] Ask God to give you this kind of love for people who need salvation.

HEROES OF OUR FAITH

RUTH

God Included Her in His Plan

The biblical character Ruth could be called "Least Likely to Succeed" if there were such a contest. She lived in Moab, a desolate land southeast of Israel. Moabites were considered outcasts for two reasons: (1) their nation began from an incestuous relationship between a man named Lot and his daughter; and (2) the Moabites refused to help the Hebrews when they attempted to enter the Promised Land God gave them. For that reason God decreed that for ten generations no Moabite could enter the Lord's assembly to worship Him.

And yet there is a small book in the Bible named after Ruth! When we first meet her Ruth is in mourning after losing her Jewish husband. When her Jewish mother-in-law, Naomi, also a widow, decides to return to Israel from Moab, Ruth begs to accompany her. Israel was no place for this young Gentile, but Ruth made a life-defining choice: she told Naomi, "Your people shall be my people, and your God, my God" (Ruth 1:16). Even though she was not a Jew, she wanted to follow the true God. And God rewarded her faith.

When Ruth and Naomi arrived in Bethlehem, God extended miraculous favor and mercy to Ruth. She met a Jewish man named Boaz, who decided to marry her, and they had a baby named Obed. That child grew up to be the grandfather of King David, which means Ruth was inserted into the royal line of Israel. In fact, her name appears in the genealogy of Jesus Christ in the Book of Matthew (1:5). Ruth's ancient story was a foreshadowing of the beautiful mercy of Christ, who made it possible for undeserving sinners and outcasts to enjoy His blessings and salvation. Her life reminds us of the words of Paul, who announced to all Gentiles in Ephesians 2:13: "But now in Christ Jesus you who formerly were far away have been brought near by the blood of Christ."

Break Every Chain

Finding Freedom From Your Past

"It does not spoil your happiness to confess your sin. The unhappiness is in not making the confession."

—CHARLES H. SPURGEON (1834–1892)
BRITISH PREACHER AND AUTHOR

W HEN JESUS BEGAN His ministry in Israel He immediately challenged people to repent of their sins. The first thing Jesus is recorded as saying in the Gospel of Mark is about repentance: "The time is fulfilled, and the kingdom of God is at hand; repent and believe in the gospel" (Mark 1:15). In Matthew, Jesus began His preaching ministry by saying: "Repent, for the kingdom of heaven is at hand" (Matthew 4:17).

After Jesus was resurrected, His disciples continued to preach a message of repentance. When Peter spoke to the crowd on the day of Pentecost, they asked him, "What shall we do?" and he said: "Repent, and each of you be baptized in the name of Jesus Christ for the forgiveness of your sins; and you will receive the gift of the Holy Spirit" (Acts 2:38).

This word *repent* is a bold and confrontational word. It means not only to turn to God, but also to turn away from sin after feeling remorse or sorrow. The word describes a powerful decision to change attitude and heart. Some people have described repentance as a 180-degree turn away from sin. Every person who follows Jesus sincerely must repent from his past or his conversion is not genuine.

There are examples in the Bible of people who had dramatic conversions and immediately stopped their sinful habits:

- Jesus visited a tax collector named Zaccheus who had become rich from stealing money. After his repentance he told Jesus he was going to pay back four times what he took from the people he defrauded (Luke 19:1–10). He totally renounced his life of greed and began giving to the poor. The selfish thief became a generous man.

- Jesus told the story of a wayward son who took his father's inheritance and wasted it by living immorally. But after he "came to his senses" (Luke 15:17) the young man returned to his father's house and apologized. Because of his repentance, he made a clean break from his past sins. The disrespectful rebel became an honorable son.

- When we first meet the apostle Paul in the Book of Acts he is a murderer and a persecutor of Christians. But after he sees a vision of Jesus on the road to Damascus, he breaks from his past and becomes a Christian himself. Paul starts helping Christians instead of attacking them.

- In the apostle Paul's first letter to the Corinthians he mentions that people in that church used to be involved in idol worship, fornication, adultery, homosexuality, stealing, alcohol abuse, and other sins. But he then says they were "washed," "sanctified," and "justified"—because they had repented of their deeds (1 Corinthians 6:11). Some of the worst sinners of Corinth began living like saints.

Some people are transformed overnight when they surrender their lives to Jesus. They throw their drugs or liquor out the window, apologize to the people they've wronged, break off unhealthy relationships, and make a total turnaround. The process of change is slower for other people. While the new birth is indeed an instantaneous experience, salvation is not. We aren't just "saved" in an emotional moment; we are "being saved" on a daily basis.

When you began your journey with Jesus, I'm sure you repented from all known sins and put your faith in Jesus. The Holy Spirit came into your heart and you experienced the miracle of conversion. But if you still struggle with certain sinful habits from your past, don't be discouraged. The same God who began this transformation in your life will finish it.

We can see this process exemplified in the story of Lazarus, a man whom Jesus raised from the dead. Lazarus had been dead for four days when Jesus arrived to see him; his body had already begun to stink.

But Jesus asked the people there to move the stone from the entrance of the tomb, and He commanded Lazarus to come out. When Lazarus emerged from the grave he was still wrapped in his graveclothes like a mummy.

At that point Jesus said to the people standing nearby: "Unbind him, and let him go" (John 11:44). This is often how it works for us. With God's help we are able to repent and put our trust in Jesus, but we need our Christian friends to help us get unwrapped from all the things that have bound us.

When people come to Christ they come to Him with all forms of brokenness.

Some are addicted to behaviors or substances; others are emotionally crippled because of their upbringing; still others are haunted by childhood trauma. Often our advice to them is, "Get over it. If you're a Christian you can't struggle with those things." But that is both insensitive and unrealistic.

Christians may struggle with sinful habits, and sometimes they may fall into temptation, but the good news is that we have access to God's amazing grace to help us overcome. Every time you repent from a sin, you receive fresh grace to be free from sin's power.

Your journey with God is a life of repentance. British preacher Charles Spurgeon said: "Sincere repentance is continual. Believers repent until their dying day."[1] We don't just repent one time when we decide to become a believer in Jesus. We may repent several times daily as the Holy Spirit convicts us of bad attitudes, wrong behaviors, or unkind words. As we learn to surrender our fleshly desires to God, He frees us from all our chains.

LET'S GO **DEEPER**

1. Repentance is called a "gift" from God in the New Testament. According to Romans 2:4, what is it that leads us to true repentance?

_____

2. How does God call us to live in 1 Peter 1:15–16?

_____

3. Read 2 Corinthians 7:1. What do we need to do to perfect holiness in our lives?

_____

_____

_____

When you hear the word *holiness*, it might trigger thoughts of a certain dress code or hairstyle or a self-righteous religious person. But holiness is not about acting spiritually superior. Holiness means, literally, to be set apart for God's use. We can "perfect holiness" in our lives by abstaining from sin and by constantly surrendering our hearts, motives, attitudes, and actions to God. Ultimately, however, we cannot be truly holy apart from God's mercy and grace.

4. Read Psalm 139:23–24. How should we pray if we want to live holy lives?

_____

_____

_____

5. Read Romans 12:1–2. What should we do so that we can please God?

_____

_____

_____

6. What happens when we confess our sins, according to 1 John 1:9?

_____

_____

_____

7. The previous passage in 1 John 1:9 refers to personal confession of sin. You can confess your sins directly to God and experience forgiveness and cleansing. But in James 5:16 a different type of confession is mentioned. What does God tell us to do in this passage, and what will happen as a result?

_____

_____

_____

LET'S **TALK** ABOUT IT

Has the Lord set you free from a sinful habit? Tell the others in your group how this happened.

Memory Verse

If we confess our sins, He is faithful and righteous to forgive us our sins and to cleanse us from all unrighteousness.

—1 John 1:9

LET'S GO EVEN DEEPER
Freedom Through Confession of Sin

We can take our sins directly to Jesus and experience forgiveness. But confession to others is also very important. When we admit our failures and sins to a brother or sister in Christ, we must swallow our pride. Confessing our sins in this way lays an axe to the root of our sins and releases spiritual healing.

If you have never done so, it is a good idea to schedule an appointment with a mentor, pastor, or mature Christian friend and confess your past sins. You don't do this to embarrass yourself but to find full freedom from shame. James 4:6 says God "gives grace to the humble." Opening your heart in transparent confession is a healthy exercise that will unleash greater grace so you can overcome sinful habits.

When you open your heart in this way, you can use the following checklist to confess any sinful habit patterns or traumatic experiences from your past.

Unforgiveness. We can't experience the true forgiveness of Jesus if we hold resentment in our hearts toward others. Bitterness is like acid. It will corrode our souls until we forgive those who hurt us. Confess it openly if you are carrying any grudges.

Fear and anxiety. Everyone has natural fears. It's normal to be afraid of snakes or spiders, for example, so we will stay away from them. But other fears are unnatural. Many people have been traumatized by past experiences such as sexual abuse, bullying, poverty, family breakup, rape, accidents, or war. The Holy Spirit can bring supernatural peace to our troubled minds and deliver us from the shackles of post-traumatic stress.

Sexual immorality. While society today says "free sex" is totally acceptable, the psychological and spiritual damage caused by fornication, abortion, homosexuality, adultery, and pornography is real. The chains of sexual sin are strong, but Jesus can shatter them when we confess our sins and choose purity. You may need to confess your sexual history so you can know you have been forgiven.

Occult involvement. Participation in any form of witchcraft (séances, fortune-telling, idol worship, horoscopes, New Age practices, or satanic covenants) will open the doors of our spirits to demonic influence.

These chains can only be broken by the power of Jesus as we confess our involvement in occultism.

Depression and grief. It is normal to grieve a loss, but sometimes we can be fixated on a negative experience and suffer from a spirit of heaviness. Depression can lead to self-hatred, eating disorders, cutting, and even suicide. Yet Jesus offers abundant life and a sustainable joy. We must talk openly about our pain and receive prayer for healing.

Addiction. People often use alcohol, nicotine, illegal drugs, or prescription medicines to numb their emotional pain. Yet the Holy Spirit can go to the root of our brokenness and heal our souls. If you are bound by a harmful habit, confess this and break free from the chains.

Father or mother wounds. Many people struggle through life because their own parents were either absent, distant, critical, abusive, or addicted to alcohol or drugs. Because the relationship with a parent is so foundational these wounds can affect the core of our being. It is liberating when we can open our hearts and receive prayer for this pain. Let the heavenly Father's love heal you.

HEROES OF OUR FAITH

STEPHEN

The Church's First Martyr

Before Jesus' execution He told His followers they would be persecuted for their faith. He said in Matthew 24:9: "Then they will deliver you to tribulation, and will kill you, and you will be hated by all nations because of My name." Even though Christians carry the gospel of hope and salvation, Satan hates this life-giving message, and he will do anything to hinder it. This is why so many Christians have died while defending their faith. We honor Stephen as the first New Testament martyr.

Stephen was a fervent preacher who was part of the original Christian church in Jerusalem. He was known as a "Hellenistic Jew"—a Greek who followed the Jewish faith. He knew the Scriptures so well that he could quote many Old Testament passages. In a powerful sermon he preached in Jerusalem, recorded in Acts 7, he mentioned Abraham, Isaac, Jacob, Joseph, Moses, David, and Solomon as he tried to convince unbelieving Jews that Jesus is the Son of God.

Luke, the author of the Book of Acts, doesn't say if anyone made a decision to follow Jesus because of Stephen's courageous sermon. In fact, Stephen didn't even get to finish it! The angry crowd went berserk. They didn't want to hear about their sin. The mob chased Stephen out of the city and stoned him—as if they could wipe out his message by killing him.

Stephen's death was tragic, but it didn't stop the early church from growing. Not only did his martyrdom scatter the disciples to all regions of Judea (thus spreading the gospel to new territories), but an angry Pharisee named Saul heard Stephen's piercing words that day. No doubt the sermon troubled him. Saul wanted to stamp out Christianity, but on his way to kill more Christians in Syria he saw a vision of Jesus and was dramatically converted. Saul eventually became known as the apostle Paul, and he continued preaching the message that Stephen died defending. Persecution can't stop the gospel.

Hearing God's Voice

How God Supernaturally Guides Us

"I don't have the strength or wisdom to get through a
single day without guidance and grace from God."
—TONY DUNGY (1955–)
FORMER NATIONAL FOOTBALL LEAGUE COACH

How do you make personal decisions? Some people rely on their own judgment. Others read self-help books, listen to podcasts, or get their friends' opinions about what choices they should make. And there are people who may read horoscopes, visit palm readers, or call psychic hotlines to get personal guidance.

But if you are a Christian the Bible says relying on your own limited knowledge, or seeking guidance from the occult, will not result in blessing. Like a good father, God wants to guide us so that we make right choices. Like a compassionate shepherd, He wants to direct us into peaceful pastures—and He longs to protect us from danger.

One of the most amazing attributes of God is His willingness to communicate. He is not silent. He loves to talk to His people. As soon as He created Adam and Eve at the beginning of time He blessed them and gave them instructions. God talked to Abraham, Isaac, and Jacob. He gave detailed messages to Moses, Elijah, and many other prophets.

In Old Testament times the Holy Spirit did not dwell inside people as He does today. So God spoke to people in various and unusual ways:

- After Job prayed a lengthy prayer, God spoke to Job and revealed His power and wisdom. Job's response was to repent of his pride and say: "I have heard of You by the hearing of the ear; but now my eye sees You" (Job 42:5).

- He appeared to Moses in a burning bush in the desert, and God called his name when Moses drew near to the fire (Exodus 3:4).

- The angel of the Lord appeared to Joshua to remind him that God was with the people of Israel as they entered the Promised Land. Joshua fell on his face as he listened to the message (Joshua 5:13–15).

- At a time when words from God were rare, the Lord audibly called the boy Samuel's name, and Samuel said, "Here I am" (1 Samuel 3:1–4). Samuel grew up to be a powerful prophet who carried God's message to many people.

- Isaiah had a vision of Jesus on the throne of heaven, and Jesus commissioned the young prophet to confront the sins of Israel (Isaiah 6:9–13).

People in the Old Testament saw visions from God, heard His audible voice, received messages from angels, or listened to God speak through prophets. God can still speak in all those ways, but something monumental happened after Jesus died and was raised from the dead. He gave us the Holy Spirit, and He promised that the Spirit would guide and direct us:

> But when He, the Spirit of truth, comes, He will guide you into all the truth; for He will not speak on His own initiative, but whatever He hears, He will speak; and He will disclose to you what is to come.
>
> —JOHN 16:13

Before the invention of digital technology people who were traveling by car had to use paper maps to get to their destinations. These maps were fairly accurate if they were updated, but it wasn't easy to look at a paper map while driving. After the invention of smartphones global navigation technology became common. Today people can listen to a digital voice that actually tells them where to turn, how long to stay on a certain highway, and even which roads to avoid because of accidents.

The Holy Spirit is much like a GPS device, except that He never makes mistakes and would never accidentally take you to the wrong address! If you are a born-again Christian, you have been blessed with the absolute best navigation system ever. The Holy Spirit convicts us when we sin, warns us of danger, guides us when we face decisions, comforts us when we are discouraged, gives wisdom when we are confused, and connects us with the people we need to know.

Yet many Christians struggle when it comes to guidance. When they pray they strain to hear anything. They know God speaks, but either they don't believe He wants to talk to them, or they don't want to obey what He says. Many believers have never known the thrill of hearing God's gentle voice in their spirits.

There are Christians who teach that God doesn't speak to people personally. They believe the only guidance you need comes from the Bible. That's a strange doctrine since the phrases "And God said..." or "the word of the Lord came to so-and-so" appear more than two thousand times in the Old Testament alone. There are four primary ways God communicates with us today:

1. You can hear God's voice by reading the Bible. God inspired forty authors over a period of sixteen hundred years to compile the Bible, and He went to a lot of trouble to give us His book. Yet today Bibles collect dust because people are too busy to read His personalized love letter to us. When you read Scripture with a prayerful heart, God can cause a verse to jump off the page as a direct message to you. This is the Holy Spirit "pointing" to a verse that applies to your situation. Expect Him to speak directly to you from Scripture.

2. You can hear God's voice through the inspiration of the Holy Spirit. The Holy Spirit is not an eerie presence that just hovers around us. He lives in every born-again Christian, and He actively speaks to us. He can do this in many ways: through dreams, visions, a sense of conviction, or—most often—through His "still, small voice" of the Spirit (1 Kings 19:12, MEV).

The Holy Spirit can give you prophetic dreams and visions, but the most common way He speaks is through a deep sense of "inward knowing." This is more like a deep mental impression. It usually comes in a moment, so that you know it did not originate with you.

The ability to hear the Spirit's voice is developed over years as we grow in Christ. If you really want to hear Him, ask God to fill you with His Spirit. (See lesson 17 in this study.) As you allow more of the Spirit's presence and power in your life, you will set aside your selfish agendas and sinful habits so God can communicate without hindrance.

3. You can hear God's voice through people. We are members of

His body, the church, and you will hear God better when you are in fellowship with His people. God can speak to you through a pastor's sermon, a friend's wise counsel, a mother's rebuke, a mentor's phone call, or a prophetic word given to you by one of God's Spirit-filled servants. If you live in total isolation, you probably won't hear much from God.

God also uses the gift of prophecy, but you should never chase after prophecies. Some Christians will travel across the country to attend a prophetic conference to get a word from God, yet they have not read the Bible in months or sat still long enough to hear from God on their own. Never treat the holy gift of prophecy like fortune-telling. When God needs to speak to you in this way, He will send His faithful messengers to you at the exact time you need it.

4. You can hear God's voice through circumstances. God is sovereign, which means He is ultimately in control of your life and the world we live in. He opens doors that no man can shut. If you have been praying to get a job at one company and suddenly get an offer at a different company, this may be God's sign that He has a better workplace for you.

If you have been praying for wisdom, He may send someone into your life who knows what you need to know. If something negative happens in your life, even a tragedy, be aware that God can even use difficult challenges to direct us. Romans 8:28 promises: "And we know that God causes all things to work together for good to those who love God, to those who are called according to His purpose."

Listen and watch carefully. Tune in to His frequency. Be willing to obey Him. He promises to guide your steps.

LET'S GO **DEEPER**

1. God describes Himself as a good shepherd in Psalm 23. Read the entire psalm. What does God promise to do for us in verses 2 and 3?

_____

_____

_____

2. Read Psalm 32:8–9. What kind of attitude should we have if we want God's guidance and counsel?

_____

_____

3. Read Proverbs 3:5–6 in the New Living Translation. What three things should we do if we want clear guidance?

_____

_____

4. Read 1 Chronicles 10:13. Why was King Saul unfaithful, and what mistake did he make when seeking guidance?

_____

_____

5. Read James 1:5–6. What should we do if we lack wisdom?

_____

_____

LET'S **TALK** ABOUT IT

Tell about a time when you felt God gave you personal guidance through an impression from the Holy Spirit.

Memory Verse

I will instruct you and teach you in the way you should go; I will counsel you with my loving eye on you.

—PSALM 32:8, NIV

HEROES OF OUR FAITH

SARAH

The Mother of Our Faith

In ancient times women suffered unimaginable marginalization and mistreatment —and barren women suffered even more because a woman's
worth was based on her fertility. Yet when we first meet Sarai in the Bible,
Genesis 11:30 says: "Sarai was barren; she had no child." In those days a
woman would have been shamed or blamed for being infertile. Yet God had
big plans for Sarai, even though she struggled to believe His promise.

God told Sarai's husband, Abram, that he would become the father of
nations. But Abram couldn't do that job by himself! Just as God needed a
man, Adam, and a woman, Eve, to populate the world, He chose a man and
a woman to start His holy nation of Israel. Even though women have been
abused and sidelined for centuries, God has always intended to use both
men and women to establish His kingdom on earth. When a woman finds
God and puts her trust in Him, He can use her in profound ways.

God changed Abram's name to Abraham, which means "father of nations," and He changed Sarai's name to Sarah, which means "my princess."
It denotes a queenly authority, which is confirmed in Genesis 17:16 when
God says of her, "She shall be a mother of nations." Sarah laughed when
she first heard that God was going to give her a child in her old age. But
a miracle happened—at age ninety she gave birth to baby Isaac. Hebrews
11:11 says Sarah "received ability to conceive, even beyond the proper time
of life, since she considered Him faithful who had promised." In spite of her
many doubts, and the many obstacles on her difficult journey, Sarah became
a model of strong faith for all who follow the true God.

He Made Them Male and Female

God's Plan for Marriage and Family

"God cares who we sleep with because he cares deeply about the people who are doing the sleeping. He cares because sex was his idea, not ours. He cares because misusing sex can inflict profound hurt and damage. He cares because he regards us as worthy of his care."

—SAM ALLBERRY (1975–)
PASTOR AND AUTHOR OF *WHY DOES GOD CARE WHO I SLEEP WITH?*

WHEN CHRISTIANITY BEGAN in the first century the Roman Empire was at its zenith. Immediately there was a cultural clash—not just because Christians refused to worship Roman emperors but also because Christian morality was so different from the behavior of the Romans. Consider what life was like in the moral darkness of ancient Rome:

- Men were considered dominant, and women had very few rights. Most women got married in their early teen years so they could have as many babies as possible; they were not valued beyond their ability to procreate.

- Marriage was common, but men were expected to be promiscuous outside of their marriage relationships while women were expected to stay faithful to their husbands.

- Homosexuality was common, and men considered it "manly" to have sex with other men and even boys as long as they were the dominant partners in the relationship. Sex was really about proving dominance.

- Because men cherished the idea of masculine superiority, rape was accepted and slaves were commonly abused sexually. Prostitution was also legal. There were few laws to protect children, slaves, or others from sexual abuse.

- Emperor Nero (who ruled during the days of the apostle Paul's travels) was a murderous sexual deviant who celebrated incest, married a man, and often hosted orgies and drunken feasts in his palace.[1]

This historical backdrop helps us understand why the Christian idea of family, marriage, and sexual integrity was at odds with the prevailing culture of the day. When the gospel began spreading to Gentile nations, the Christian idea of sexual purity or fidelity was a foreign concept. And yet as the early disciples preached about the salvation of Jesus, they also taught Greeks, Romans, Arabs, and people from many other nations that God had a revolutionary new code of sexual behavior.

The apostle Paul wrote letters to these Gentiles in places such as Rome (in Italy); Corinth, Philippi, and Thessalonica (in Greece); and Ephesus (a headquarters of immoral idolatry in what is now Turkey). In each of these places a pagan view of sexuality was the norm. That means people commonly practiced adultery, fornication (unmarried sex), rape, incest, group sex, homosexuality, pedophilia, and ritual prostitution.

Can you imagine how challenging it was for first-century Christians to teach converts a whole new way to look at sex? Yet this is exactly what the apostle Paul did when he wrote to the Romans. He said:

> The night is almost gone, and the day is near. Therefore let us lay aside the deeds of darkness and put on the armor of light. Let us behave properly as in the day, not in carousing and drunkenness, not in sexual promiscuity and sensuality, not in strife and jealousy.
> —ROMANS 13:12–13

In almost every letter Paul wrote to the early churches he called for sexual purity and asked his new disciples to abstain from the old immoral practices. Paul taught that when a man or woman finds Christ they become a new creature (2 Corinthians 5:17). Paul called followers of Jesus to put aside the old behaviors and adopt the sexuality of Christ's kingdom. He didn't leave them any room for compromise in this area. This meant:

We should be faithful to one sexual partner. The New Testament affirms what the Old Testament taught centuries ago—that God's plan for marriage is *one man and one woman*. This is revealed in the relationship between Adam and Eve in the first chapter of Genesis. The Bible teaches that we should find one marriage partner and enjoy a committed sexual relationship with that spouse, instead of engaging in endless encounters with multiple people. This revolutionary idea of monogamy requires mutual respect, trust, faithfulness, and selfless love. Marriage also creates the safe and stable environment in which to raise children.

Men should respect and cherish their wives, not dominate them. Paul called men to treat their wives as equals, which was diametrically opposed to the Roman concepts of masculine domination and cruelty. The New Testament also clarifies that God does not endorse polygamy, which was common in the first century. The practice of having multiple wives devalues and degrades women; monogamy allows a husband and wife to enjoy equality and intimacy.

God created two genders. The true God created men and women because both genders together reflect His image. God's full glory is not evident through men or women alone. Both are required. That's why Genesis 1:27 says: "So God created human beings in his own image. In the image of God he created them; male and female he created them" (NLT). The Bible does not teach that gender is fluid or changeable. And the apostle Paul taught that it is sinful for men to be "effeminate," a word used in 1 Corinthians 6:9 that implies twisting or perverting fixed gender.

God does not sanction sex outside of marriage. To protect us, God drew loving boundaries around our sexuality. In the Old and New Testaments God forbids fornication (sex between unmarried people), adultery (when a married person engages in sex with a different partner), homosexuality, incest, bestiality, sexual perversion, and rape. God didn't give us these guidelines to deny us pleasure; there is plenty of pleasure in married sex. But if we put our pursuit of sexual pleasure above our desire to love and please God, we end up separating ourselves from Him.

Our culture today is really not that different from ancient Rome. Many unmarried people live together and consider marriage old-fashioned. Divorce is common (and in some cases it can't be avoided because of adultery, abuse, or other sinful behaviors). Same-sex marriage is accepted and celebrated, as is any other form of homosexual behavior. Pornography of every genre is widely available. Human trafficking is a multibillion-dollar industry because there is a global appetite for prostitution.[2] And more and more, people are making the decision to identify with a different gender or even undergo surgery or inject hormones to alter their gender characteristics.

As Christians we can't change biblical views of sexuality to accommodate people's behaviors. God's Word can't be rewritten to conform to cultural trends. However, we must show love and kindness to all people, regardless of whether they are gay, bisexual, transgender, or living with an unmarried partner. Our job is not to judge or shame people but to introduce them to a relationship with Jesus. When they begin a relationship with Him, He will change them from the inside and give them the power to be sexually pure.

LET'S GO **DEEPER**

1. What does God say about marriage in Hebrews 13:4?

_____

_____

2. Read 1 Corinthians 6:9–11. List the ten types of people who will not inherit the kingdom of God.

_____   _____

_____   _____

_____   _____

_____   _____

_____   _____

3. Even though these people deserved God's judgment, what happened to them in verse 11?

_____

_____

186

4. Read 1 Corinthians 6:18. How should we respond when we face the temptation to commit immorality?

_____

5. Based on 1 Corinthians 6:18, why is it important to resist sexual sin?

_____

6. Read 1 Thessalonians 4:3. What is God's will for our lives?

_____

7. Read 1 Thessalonians 4:4–8. For what purpose has God called us?

_____

8. Read Galatians 5:24. What does Paul say we must do with our lustful passions? How do we do this?

_____

_____

_____

LET'S **TALK** ABOUT IT

Christians are often accused of "hate speech" if we don't agree with someone's sexual choices. How would you respond if you were accused of "hating" because you hold to a biblical view of sexuality?

Memory Verse

Flee from youthful lusts and pursue righteousness, faith, love and peace, with those who call on the Lord from a pure heart.

—2 Timothy 2:22

HEROES OF OUR FAITH

TITUS
A Next-Generation Apostle

We don't know when and where Titus became a Christian, but we know the apostle Paul led this Greek man to faith and considered him a spiritual son. Paul refers to Titus as "my true child in a common faith" in the short epistle that bears Titus' name (Titus 1:4). But Paul also referred to Titus as "my partner and fellow worker" in 2 Corinthians 8:23. Titus must have grown so fast spiritually—and displayed so much faithfulness and strong character—that Paul brought him into his inner circle and trusted him to carry out his work.

Paul couldn't be everywhere. He needed leaders who could handle the tough challenges of planting the seed of the gospel in new territories. Eventually Paul commissioned Titus to oversee the churches that had been planted in Crete, an island off the southern coast of Greece. Like Timothy, Silas, Epaphras, and others, Titus was part of a new generation of young leaders who were equipped to carry the torch after pioneers like Paul, Peter, and John finished their race.

Titus also represented the multicultural future of the New Testament church. The first Christians were Jews, but Paul continually reminded Jewish-Christian leaders that the gospel wasn't for Jews only. Titus was obvious proof of this. When Paul brought Titus to Jerusalem, some rigid legalists wanted to force Titus to be circumcised to conform to outdated Jewish rules. (See Galatians 2:1-3.) But Paul rebuked these men for putting old covenant rituals in front of the grace we received in Jesus Christ.

Paul used Titus as a vivid reminder that the Holy Spirit wants to reach people from all ethnic backgrounds. The last time we hear about Titus, in Paul's second letter to Timothy, Titus was preaching the gospel in Dalmatia, which is part of modern Croatia. If young Christians are properly mentored, they will break barriers and extend Christ's kingdom in surprising ways.

Blessed to Multiply

How to Become a Disciple Maker

"Jesus told us to do more than just get converts. He told us to make disciples."
—LEROY EIMS (1925-2004)
AUTHOR WHO SERVED WITH THE NAVIGATORS FOR MORE THAN FIFTY YEARS

WHEN JESUS BEGAN His ministry He didn't rent a coliseum for an evangelistic campaign or put billboards all over Jerusalem announcing His healing ministry. He did sometimes preach to crowds, but the first thing He did was gather a group of close followers. They were called "disciples," which means "taught ones."

Mark 3:14 says Jesus appointed His twelve disciples "so that they would be with Him and that He could send them out to preach." Notice that His relationship with them was not just about the work. He was not just recruiting followers to perform a task. He wanted their fellowship first— and then He let them preach what they learned from Him.

This was Jesus' method of ministry. He didn't focus on quantity. He wanted quality, so He made the few His priority. He ate with them, lived with them, and traveled the dusty roads of Galilee with them. Even when He did mass meetings, He used these gatherings to instruct the disciples so they would one day preach like Him.

For three and a half years Jesus invested in His closest followers in a deeply personal way—not as an instructor in a clinical sense, but as a friend. Jesus did not mass-produce legions of followers. He hand-carved a few—and they became the pillars of the early church.

Jesus was not the first character in the Bible to model this method of personal discipleship. In Old Testament times Moses trained Joshua to be his successor, Naomi mentored Ruth to follow the true God, and Elijah mentored Elisha and gave him a double portion of his power. There was a long tradition of mentorship in Hebrew culture.

Aside from mentoring His twelve male disciples, Jesus also mentored a group of women who became some of His bravest witnesses. Then, when it was time for Him to leave this earth, Jesus commissioned the small group of people He had trained to do what He did. Just before ascending into heaven He told them: "Go therefore and make disciples of all the nations" (Matthew 28:19).

Notice that Jesus did not say, "Go therefore and make converts," "Go therefore and gather crowds," or "Go therefore and build churches," even though those things aren't wrong. His mandate was very specific. Jesus wants His disciples to multiply.

Jesus' disciples took this mandate seriously. Each of them personally invested in training others, and this process triggered exponential growth in the early church. When one Christian personally mentors another convert, and that convert becomes a strong believer, then you have two strong believers. Those two then make four disciples; then four make eight. Eight strong believers then produce sixteen. And the process continues until there are millions.

Making disciples was the apostle Paul's central focus too. The Book of Acts describes when Paul first met his disciple Timothy (Acts 16:1–3) and how Timothy was eventually appointed as an apostolic leader in Ephesus. Paul invested his life in this one young man, and he was so proud of him that he told the Philippians, "I have no one else of kindred spirit who will genuinely be concerned for your welfare" (Philippians 2:20). Paul poured so much of himself into Timothy that Timothy became like a junior version of his mentor—only with his own unique personality and spiritual strengths.

This simple but profound principle was best explained by Paul when he commissioned Timothy to spread the gospel. Paul said:

> The things which you have heard from me in the presence of many witnesses, entrust these to faithful men who will be able to teach others also.
>
> —2 Timothy 2:2

This is what some people call "The 222 Principle." God can do a powerful miracle when one Christian disciples another person. Paul told Timothy to focus his attention on a few faithful followers; when those people became mature disciples, they would then be able to disciple others. Although this process might seem slow and tedious at first, imagine how many people could be discipled in forty years! What starts small eventually explodes.

This mandate given to Timothy is yours as well. Discipleship is not just a job for full-time pastors or traveling evangelists. Every Christian is called to reproduce spiritually. The job description of a disciple maker is simple:

- **Identify** the people you are called to mentor. They may ask you to disciple them, or you may be led by the Holy Spirit to invite someone to a Bible study or small group. Let God show you the people you should spend time with.

- **Invest** your time in these people by meeting with them, answering questions, counseling, and sharing from your own life experiences.

- **Include** your disciples when you do ministry so they can learn from watching you. Invite them to help you, and give them opportunities to pray for people, share testimonies, or teach. Pushing them out of their comfort zones will help them grow.

- **Instruct** your disciples from God's Word. Help them develop a daily habit of Bible study and prayer, and do Bible studies with them.

- **Intercede** for your disciples regularly. Pray for their special needs, and pray that they will grow spiritually.

Now that you have reached the end of this study it's time to decide how you will help other believers mature in their Christian faith. This could happen in many different ways. You might lead someone to Christ at your school, your workplace, or while conversing with them on social media. After you pray with them you could invite them to do the *Let's Go Deeper* Bible study with you or study a book of the Bible together.

Or you might meet an immature or lapsed Christian who was never discipled. You can invite him or her to a Bible study with a small group or just meet with them one-on-one on a weekly basis. You may also plan an online Bible study for people you know who don't live in your area.

Relational discipleship takes a lot of time and energy, but investing your life in others is one of the most fulfilling experiences in life. Once you have poured your life into another brother or sister, and watched them mature in Christ, you will grow in your leadership skills, your disciples will begin to mentor others, and you will watch the multiplication process unfold. This is when the Christian adventure really gets exciting.

LET'S GO **DEEPER**

1. When Jesus called Peter, Andrew, and John to be His disciples, what did He say would happen to them in Mark 1:17? What does this mean?

_____

_____

_____

2. True disciples are not casual believers who follow Jesus when they feel like it, or when it is convenient. How did Jesus describe a serious, committed disciple in Luke 9:23–24?

_____

_____

_____

Jesus said certain things would prove that we are His true disciples. Look up these scriptures, and write down the qualities of a genuine disciple:

3. John 8:31–32

_____

4. John 13:34–35

_____

5. John 15:8

_____

6. Read 1 Thessalonians 2:10–12. The apostle Paul spent much time investing in his disciples in Thessalonica. How did he instruct them, and what was his goal when he mentored them?

_____

_____

_____

7. Jesus commissioned His followers to make disciples in Matthew 28:19–20. This is what we call the Great Commission. What are we supposed to teach our disciples? And what promise does Jesus give us as we make disciples?

_____

_____

_____

LET'S **TALK** ABOUT IT

Why is it more effective for us to make a few quality disciples than to focus all our attention on crowds?

Memory Verse

My Father is glorified by this, that you bear much fruit, and so prove to be My disciples.

—JOHN 15:8

A Final Word

I WAS INSPIRED TO write this Bible study after I led an Indian man to Jesus in a convenience store in 2020. He didn't have a Bible, and as we talked more, I realized he didn't have much knowledge of Bible stories or Christian concepts. So I tried to summarize the principles of my faith in the simplest form possible so he could grow spiritually.

During the writing process I realized there are so many people who need a simple explanation of Christianity. God's love for us is not complicated! I hope you have found *Let's Go Deeper* helpful and encouraging.

Now that you've completed this study, you're well on your way to spiritual maturity. But your adventure of knowing Jesus has just started. I hope you will share with others what you've learned. There are so many ways you can do that!

You can organize a small group study or just meet regularly with one person and go through each lesson in this book. Discipleship doesn't have to happen inside a church building. When I was mentoring my Indian friend, we sat at a table in the back of his store and drank coffee while we read the Bible together. Sometimes I even got behind the counter of the gas station so I could show him Bible verses.

You can meet with your disciples over breakfast, in a dorm or library on campus, in your home, at the gym, in an office, or under a tree at a city park. You can also meet with people online via social media and video conferencing apps. The important thing is that you show Christ's love to your disciples and help them grow in the knowledge of God.

Long ago the Hebrew prophet Ezekiel had a vision of a huge river flowing from the temple in Jerusalem. The river started as a tiny trickle from under the building, but it grew into a wider and deeper stream. An angel appeared and began to measure the depths of the water, and it went from ankle-deep to knee-deep to waist-deep, until it became, in Ezekiel's words, "too deep to walk across. It was deep enough to swim in, but too deep to walk through" (Ezekiel 47:5, NLT).

This majestic river of God began flowing in Jerusalem, where Jesus died for us and gave us the free gift of salvation. The river represents the life of the Holy Spirit that He offers each of us. You can stay in the shallow waters—and many Christians do this—but Jesus beckons us to come deeper. I hope this study has inspired you to swim to the deepest part.

Each day, we have an opportunity to venture out deeper to explore His goodness and to allow Him to use us to touch others with His love. Don't ever stop growing spiritually. And don't ever stop bringing others with you to experience the depths of God's love for us.

—J. LEE GRADY

Answer Key

LESSON 1

Perfect and All-Powerful: The Awesome Nature of the True God

1. He is a compassionate Father.
2. He is the Lord Most High. He is the sovereign and supreme Lord of all heaven and earth.
3. He is the Lord God, the Almighty. There is no limit to His power. He is above all other gods.
4. He is the everlasting God, which means He has no end. He is also the Creator of the ends of the earth. He made all things.
5. He is judge, lawgiver, and King. He rules supremely with perfect justice.
6. He is eternal (will live forever), immortal (has no beginning or end), invisible (cannot be seen by us), and wise (has all wisdom and all knowledge).

LESSON 2

He's a Tender, Loving Father: The Amazing Character of God

1. In response, we will give thanks to God for the way He made us.
2. He is merciful, gracious, slow to anger, abundant in loving-kindness, and true (which also means faithful).
3. He is a compassionate father who extends love and compassion to us, even when we run away from Him or dishonor Him. His love is unconditional.
4. God's amazing love is impossibly broad, long, high, and deep, yet He wants us to fully know Him.

LESSON 3

Father, Son, and Holy Spirit: The Wondrous Mystery of the Trinity

1. The Holy Spirit descended upon Jesus, and the Father spoke a blessing over the Son.

2. The Father sent the Holy Spirit into our hearts so we can know we are adopted by God.

3. Jesus said He would send the Holy Spirit, and the Spirit would proceed from the Father. The Holy Spirit will then testify about Jesus.

4. Jesus was anointed by the Holy Spirit so He could heal people and free them from demons.

5. The Father knows us, the Holy Spirit sanctifies us (or cleanses us), and the Son, Jesus Christ, sprinkles us with His blood to forgive us.

LESSON 4

Lost in Total Darkness: The Problem of Man's Sinfulness

1. Greed, evil, envy, murder, strife, deceit, malice, gossip, slander, hatred of God, insolence, arrogance, boasting, inventing evil, disobedience to parents, having no understanding, untrustworthiness, a lack of love, a lack of mercy, and approval of people who do wicked things.

2. The intent of men's thoughts is to do evil continually.

3. All men have turned away from God to live their own way.

4. God saw that all men turned away and became corrupt. There is no man who does good.

LESSON 5

What a Glorious Savior: Who Is Jesus Christ?

1. The angel said Jesus will save His people from their sins.
2. Jesus went everywhere doing good, healing people and setting them free from the devil's power.
3. Jesus came to earth to be the Savior of the world.
4. Jesus is the mediator between God and man. A mediator is one who negotiates peace between two parties that are in conflict.
5. Jesus abolished death and brought us life and immortality.
6. Jesus is both Lord and Christ.
7. Jesus is called King of kings and Lord of lords.

LESSON 6

The Incarnation Miracle: How Jesus Is Both God and Man

1. A virgin will bear a child, and He will be called Immanuel, which means "God with us."
2. The angel said the child in Mary's womb had been conceived by the Holy Spirit and that He will be named Jesus because He will save the people from their sins.
3. The child will be born, and the government (or the kingdom) will rest on His shoulders. He will be called "Wonderful Counselor, Mighty God, Eternal Father, [and] Prince of Peace."
4. Even though He was God, He emptied Himself and took on the form of a bond servant, made in the likeness of men.
5. Jesus was still fully God even when He was in the likeness of a man. Jesus had to be fully God and fully man in order to give His life as a sacrifice for our sins.

LESSON 7

The Greatest Moment in History: How Jesus Saved Us on the Cross

1. First Jesus asked the Father to take the cup of suffering from Him. But then He said, "Yet not what I will, but what You will." He surrendered to the difficult task of suffering for us.

2. Jesus gave Himself for our sins to rescue us from this evil age.

3. Jesus reconciled us to God.

4. He redeemed us with His precious blood.

5. He obtained eternal redemption with His own blood.

6. He forgives our sins and cleanses us from all unrighteousness.

LESSON 8

Death Is Defeated: The Power of Christ's Resurrection

1. Peter didn't want Jesus to die. He told Jesus, "God forbid it, Lord! This shall never happen to You!"

2. Jesus said He was going to be handed over to the chief priests and that He would be condemned to death, mocked, flogged, and crucified. But He also said He would be raised from the dead.

3. The angel told the women not to be afraid. He said to them: "He is not here, for He has risen, just as He said. Come, see the place where He was lying. Go quickly and tell His disciples that He has risen from the dead; and behold, He is going ahead of you into Galilee, there you will see Him; behold, I have told you."

4. Jesus said to Thomas, "Because you have seen Me, have you believed? Blessed are they who did not see, and yet believed."

5. Jesus appeared to Cephas (Peter), then to the other disciples, then to more than five hundred other people, then to James,

then again to all the apostles. Finally, Jesus appeared to Saul when he was on the road to Damascus.

6. Paul said, "And if Christ has not been raised, your faith is worthless; you are still in your sins." Everything we believe as Christians hinges on the truth of the resurrection.

LESSON 9

You Must Be Born Again: The Miracle of Spiritual Conversion

1. We were dead in our transgressions and sins.

2. We must confess with our mouths that Jesus is Lord, and believe in our hearts that God raised Him from the dead.

3. We are born again because of the imperishable seed of the Word of God.

4. Jesus is the source of salvation. Only in His name can we be saved. We must believe in the name of Jesus Christ.

5. When we are in Christ, we become new creatures. The old things from our past go away and everything becomes new.

6. *Eternal life* is knowing God and Jesus Christ personally.

LESSON 10

Buried With Christ: Why We Need Water Baptism

1. When we are baptized, we are buried with Christ into death and then raised from the dead so we can walk in newness of life. In baptism we are united with Jesus in His death and resurrection. We are reminded that our old selves have been crucified with Christ so we are no longer slaves to sin.

2. In baptism we are buried with Christ and then raised up with Him. We were dead in our sins, but in baptism we are made alive together with Christ because we have been forgiven for all our sins.

3. When we are baptized in water, we are clothed with Christ.

4. We are instructed here not to delay following Jesus in baptism. Baptism is a step of obedience to God. Baptism is a powerful declaration that our sins have been washed away.

LESSON 11

The Greatest Book of All: Why Christians Cherish the Bible

1. Our ways will be established, and we will not be ashamed.

2. We will keep our ways pure.

3. We will not sin against God.

4. We will get understanding, and we will hate every false way.

5. God's Word will be a lamp to our feet and a light to our paths. We will experience God's guidance.

6. God's Word gives us light and understanding.

7. Our footsteps will be established, and iniquity (sin) will not have dominion over us.

8. God's Word is sharp like a sword, and it can judge the thoughts and intentions of our hearts. This means the Word will reveal any sin in our lives so we can repent of it and overcome it.

9. God's Word will teach us, reprove us, correct us, and train us in righteousness so we can be equipped for good works.

10. It is not enough to hear God's Word. We must carefully observe it and obey it.

LESSON 12

The Law in Our Hearts: Why God Made a New Covenant

1. In the new covenant, God takes the law that He gave us and writes it on our hearts. It is no longer just about willpower

or external obedience but about an internal change in our hearts.

2. We are saved not by our own works but by God's grace. This miraculous grace is a gift from God that we do not deserve.

3. Jesus condemned sin in the flesh when He offered Himself to die for our sins.

4. We can approach God boldly and with confidence. We do not have to be ashamed, because we have received God's grace.

5. We can immediately go to our Advocate, Jesus. He is there to forgive and restore us if we sin.

LESSON 13

The Enemy of Our Souls: Who Exactly Is the Devil?

1. The devil is described as "the prince of the power of the air, of the spirit that is now working in the sons of disobedience."

2. The devil (who is called "the god of this world") blinds the minds of the unbelieving so they might not see the light of the gospel.

3. The devil is called a "murderer," and there is no truth in him. He is also called "a liar and the father of lies."

4. Satan's kingdom is described as "rulers," "powers," "world forces of this darkness," and "spiritual forces of wickedness in the heavenly places."

5. The full armor of God includes

- "truth" (which girds our loins, like undergarments),
- "the breastplate of righteousness,"
- the shoes of "preparation of the gospel of peace,"
- "the shield of faith,"
- "the helmet of salvation," and
- "the sword of the Spirit, which is the word of God."

6. One of Satan's tactics is to lead us astray from the simplicity and purity of devotion to Christ.

7. Satan is described as an adversary who "prowls around like a roaring lion, seeking" to devour us. We must be of sober spirit and on the alert, and we must resist him.

LESSON 14

The Gift of Eternal Life: What the Bible Says About Heaven and Hell

1. We know that we have eternal life because we love other Christians.

2. Of course we still will experience a natural death, but the phrase "never die" means we will have eternal life after we die.

3. Hell was prepared for the devil and his angels.

4. The people who will suffer eternal judgment are "those who do not know God and...those who do not obey the gospel of our Lord Jesus."

5. Hell is described as a place that is "away from the presence of the Lord and from the glory of His power."

6. The great multitude of redeemed people in heaven are standing before the throne of Jesus, clothed in white robes, waving palm branches and shouting praises to God.

7. When Christians are absent from their bodies, they will be in the Lord's presence in heaven.

8. "We know that when He appears, we will be like Him, because we will see Him just as He is."

9. First, the Lord Himself will descend from heaven with a shout. The dead in Christ will rise first; then we who are alive and remain will be caught up together with them in the clouds to meet the Lord in the air, and so we shall always be with the Lord.

10. When Jesus returns to earth, those who are alive will be changed. We will receive new, imperishable bodies. "For this perishable must put on the imperishable, and this mortal must put on immortality."

11. The last enemy to be destroyed is death.

LESSON 15

Why Do We Need the Church? Finding Your Place in God's Family

1. God's presence will be with us, even when there are only two or three people gathered.

2. Jesus Christ is the cornerstone of the building.

3. The apostles and prophets are the foundation of the building. (Many scholars believe this is a reference to the people who wrote the Old and New Testaments, since the truth of the Bible is certainly our foundation. "Apostles and prophets" can also refer to leaders of the church.)

4. The church is growing into a holy temple in the Lord.

5. We function as "one body," even though we are made up of many people.

6. Jesus is the "head of the body, the church."

7. Be devoted to one another in brotherly love, and give preference to one another in honor.

8. Be kind to one another, tenderhearted, forgiving one another.

9. Love one another.

10. Regard one another as more important than ourselves.

11. Clothe ourselves with humility toward one another.

12. Encourage one another and build up one another.

13. Confess our sins to one another, and pray for one another so we may be healed.

LESSON 16

Let's Celebrate the Feast: Why We Take the Lord's Supper

1. Jesus said we should take Communion "as often as you drink it." In other words, He did not specify a frequency.

2. When we eat the Lord's Supper, we proclaim the Lord's death until He comes. In other words, we are preaching the gospel of salvation in Christ.

3. Verse 28 says, "But a man must examine himself, and in so doing he is to eat of the bread and drink of the cup." Before taking Communion, we should examine our hearts, repent of any known sin, and approach the Lord's table with reverence.

4. Jesus promised those who eat the "bread which came down out of heaven" that they will live forever.

LESSON 17

Living in the Overflow: How to Be Filled With the Holy Spirit

1. Jesus compared the Holy Spirit to "rivers of living water."

2. Jesus said His followers would cast out demons in His name, speak with new tongues, pick up serpents or drink deadly poison and not be harmed, and lay hands on the sick and see them recover.

3. Jesus said His disciples would be "baptized with the Holy Spirit."

4. The disciples "began to speak the word of God with boldness."

5. The Holy Spirit fell upon the Gentile believers. They began to speak in tongues and exalt God.

6. Paul did not rely on persuasive words of wisdom but on the demonstration of the Holy Spirit and of power.

7. We must stay filled with the Holy Spirit.

LESSON 18

Becoming Close to Jesus: How to Pursue Intimacy With the Lord

1. We should love the Lord with all our hearts and with all our souls and with all our minds and with all our strength.

2. Eternal life is knowing God and Jesus Christ. The purpose of life is to have a relationship with God.

3. David thirsted for God. His soul and his flesh yearned for God.

4. We love God because He first loved us. He initiated this relationship.

5. God will listen when we pray, and we will find Him when we search for Him with all our hearts.

6. He will come to us like the rain, like the spring rain watering the earth.

LESSON 19

This Is Why We Sing: Cultivating a Life of Worship

1. Sing to the Lord

2. Shout joyfully to the Lord

3. Clap our hands

4. Bow to the Lord in reverence

5. Kneel before the Lord

6. Dance before the Lord

7. We must earnestly seek God and have a spiritual thirst for His presence.

8. We should praise Him as long as we live. Praise and worship should be a lifelong experience.

9. We should bless the Lord "at all times" and "continually."

10. The saints in heaven are declaring, "Hallelujah! For the Lord our God, the Almighty, reigns."

LESSON 20

Fighting the Good Fight: How to Resist Temptation

1. We are now seated with Christ in the heavenly places.
2. The law of the spirit of life in Christ Jesus has set us free from the law of sin and death.
3. God promises to provide the way of escape from temptation so we will be able to endure it.
4. We are tempted when we are carried away and enticed by our own lust.
5. Jesus said to the devil, "It is written." He quoted the Word of God to the devil.
6. If we walk by the Spirit, we will not carry out the desire of the flesh.
7. Those who belong to Christ Jesus have crucified the flesh with its passions and desires.

LESSON 21

The God Who Hears Us: Discover the Power of Prayer

1. Like the judge in the parable, God responds to persistence. He will answer us if we continue to pray night and day. We should not stop praying just because we don't get an instant answer.
2. Jesus promised that if we keep asking, He will answer; if we keep seeking, we will find; and if we keep knocking, He will open the door.
3. Jabez prayed: "Oh that You would bless me indeed and enlarge my border, and that Your hand might be with me,

and that You would keep me from harm that it may not pain me!"

4. The apostle Paul says we should be "devoted to prayer." Some translations say "constant in prayer." When we pray, we don't give up!

5. When we don't know how to pray, the Holy Spirit intercedes for us with groanings too deep for words. This means the Spirit prays within us.

6. Jesus promised that if two of us agree on earth about anything we may ask, it shall be done for us by the Father.

LESSON 22

Living in the Supernatural: Experience the Gifts of the Holy Spirit

1. All the gifts of the Holy Spirit are for "the common good" of the church.

2. Paul told Timothy not to neglect the spiritual gifts he had received.

3. The spiritual gifts mentioned in Romans 12:6–8 are

   - prophecy,

   - service,

   - teaching,

   - exhortation,

   - giving,

   - leadership, and

   - mercy.

4. He was glad he spoke in tongues privately, but in the church he said he would rather "speak five words with my mind so that I may instruct others also, rather than ten thousand words in a tongue."

5. Paul said love was more important than prophecies, tongues, knowledge, generosity to the poor, or even martyrdom.

LESSON 23

You Are Under Construction: How God Changes Us From the Inside

1. The Holy Spirit is responsible for this transformation process.
2. The new self is "in the likeness of God," and it "has been created in righteousness and holiness of the truth."
3. God promises that He will "purify the sons of Levi and refine them like gold and silver, so that they may present to the LORD offerings in righteousness."
4. We will be able to prove what the will of God is—what is good and acceptable and perfect.

LESSON 24

Digging for Divine Truth: How to Study the Bible

1. Paul said the Word of God cannot be imprisoned. Other translations say "chained." Nothing can stop God's Word from spreading.
2. Paul said they should give attention to the public reading of Scripture. This was at a time when people did not have their own Bibles, as we do today.
3. Ezra "set his heart to study the law of the LORD and to practice it, and to teach His statutes and ordinances in Israel."
4. If we accept the sayings in the Bible, we will have long life, our steps will not be impeded, we will not stumble, and God's instruction will guard us.

LESSON 25

Our Wilderness Journey: Staying Strong During Tests and Trials

1. We should not be surprised that we are experiencing trials, but we should keep rejoicing.

2. Peter said after we have suffered for a little while, "the God of all grace, who called you to His eternal glory in Christ, will Himself perfect, confirm, strengthen and establish you."

3. Our sufferings produce perseverance, which produces proven character, which produces hope.

4. In the day of trouble, David said, "He will conceal me in His tabernacle; in the secret place of His tent He will hide me; He will lift me up on a rock. And now my head will be lifted up above my enemies around me."

5. When he faced difficulties, David offered up shouts of joy and sang.

6. When we suffer, Peter said, we should entrust our souls to a faithful Creator in doing what is right.

7. We should consider it all joy when we encounter trials. These trials will produce endurance in our lives.

LESSON 26

God's Global Mission: Why We Must Spread the Gospel

1. God doesn't want anyone to perish. He wants everyone to come to repentance.

2. The disciples received boldness to preach the Word.

3. Paul was "preaching the kingdom of God and teaching concerning the Lord Jesus Christ with all openness, unhindered."

4. We should not be ashamed of the gospel.

5. Paul describes our job as that of an ambassador. And we are supposed to tell people, "We beg you on behalf of Christ, be reconciled to God."

6. Paul told Timothy that God has not given us a spirit of timidity. Therefore, he challenged Timothy not to be ashamed of the Lord and to be willing to suffer for the gospel.

LESSON 27

Break Every Chain: Finding Freedom From Your Past

1. The kindness of God leads us to repentance.

2. We are called to be holy, because God is holy.

3. We must "cleanse ourselves from all defilement of flesh and spirit."

4. We should pray, "Search me, O God, and know my heart; try me and know my anxious thoughts; and see if there be any hurtful way in me, and lead me in the everlasting way."

5. To please God, we should present our bodies as living and holy sacrifices, acceptable to God, which is our spiritual service of worship. And we should not be conformed to this world but be transformed by the renewing of our minds.

6. "If we confess our sins, [the Lord] is faithful and righteous to forgive us our sins and to cleanse us from all unrighteousness."

7. If we confess our sins to one another, we will be healed.

LESSON 28

Hearing God's Voice: How God Supernaturally Guides Us

1. He will make me lie down in green pastures, He will lead me beside quiet waters, He will restore my soul, and He will guide me in the paths of righteousness.
2. We must have a willing, submissive, and obedient attitude—not like a rebellious horse or mule that requires a bit and bridle.
3. We must trust the Lord, not depend on our own understanding, and seek God's will.
4. Saul was unfaithful because he did not obey God's word, and he sought guidance from a medium instead of from God.
5. If we lack wisdom, we should ask God, and He will generously supply us with wisdom.

LESSON 29

He Made Them Male and Female: God's Plan for Marriage and Family

1. Marriage is to be held in honor among all, and the marriage bed is to be undefiled. God says He will judge fornicators and adulterers.
2. God says these types of people will not inherit His kingdom if they do not repent of their behavior:

   - fornicators
   - idolaters
   - adulterers
   - the effeminate
   - homosexuals
   - thieves

- covetous people

- drunkards

- revilers

- swindlers

3. They were "washed," "sanctified," and "justified" because they came to know Christ. It is possible to be forgiven and cleansed of these sins.

4. When faced with sexual temptation, we are to "flee immorality." This means to quickly run from it.

5. We should flee immorality because sexual sin is a sin against our own bodies.

6. God's will for us is to live sanctified lives and abstain from immoral behavior.

7. God has not called us to sexual impurity but to sanctification.

8. We must crucify our flesh with its passions and desires.

LESSON 30

Blessed to Multiply: How to Become a Disciple Maker

1. Jesus told Peter, Andrew, and John, "Follow Me, and I will make you become fishers of men." This means He would use them to influence many people with the gospel through evangelism and discipleship.

2. A true disciple must deny himself, take up his cross, follow Jesus, and be willing to lose his life. Discipleship requires radical commitment.

3. We will be disciples of Jesus if we continue in His Word.

4. We will be disciples of Jesus if we have love for one another.

5. We will be disciples of Jesus if we bear much fruit.

6. Paul exhorted, encouraged, and implored his disciples in Thessalonica as a father would his own children, and his goal

was that they would "walk in a manner worthy of the God who calls you into His own kingdom and glory."

7. We are to teach our disciples to observe all that Jesus commanded. Then Jesus promised He would be with us until the end of the age.

Notes

LESSON 1

1. Andrew Janiak, ed., *Isaac Newton: Philosophical Writings* (Cambridge, UK: Cambridge University Press, 2014), 111.
2. "What is the Meaning of the Divine Name Yahweh?," NIV, accessed January 21, 2022, https://www.thenivbible.com/blog/what-does-yahweh-mean-in-the-bible/.

LESSON 3

1. "The Nicene Creed," Anglicans Online, accessed January 20, 2022, http://anglicansonline.org/basics/nicene.html.
2. C. S. Lewis, *Mere Christianity* (New York: HarperCollins, 2012), 162.
3. A. W. Tozer, *The Knowledge of the Holy* (San Francisco: HarperOne, 1978).

LESSON 4

1. Charles H. Spurgeon, *The Metropolitan Tabernacle Pulpit: Sermons Preached and Revised by C. H. Spurgeon in the Year 1875, vol. XXI* (London: Passmore & Alabaster, 1876), 365.

LESSON 6

1. Blue Letter Bible, s.v. *"skēnoō,"* accessed January 4, 2022, https://www.blueletterbible.org/lexicon/g4637/kjv/tr/0-1/.
2. "Jefferson's Religious Beliefs," The Jefferson Monticello, accessed January 20, 2022, https://www.monticello.org/site/research-and-collections/jeffersons-religious-beliefs.
3. Blue Letter Bible, s.v. *"episkiazō,"* accessed January 4, 2022, https://www.blueletterbible.org/lexicon/g1982/kjv/tr/0-1/.
4. R. T. Kendall, "The Stigma of Jesus' Virgin Birth," Charisma News, December 24, 2013, https://www.charismanews.com/opinion/42208-the-stigma-of-jesus-s-virgin-birth?showall=1.
5. "The Nicene Creed," Anglicans Online, accessed January 20, 2022, http://anglicansonline.org/basics/nicene.html.

LESSON 7

1. *American Dictionary of the English Language*, s.v. "redemption," accessed January 4, 2022, http://www.webstersdictionary1828.com/Dictionary/redemption.
2. Laura Geggel, "Jesus Wasn't the Only Man to Be Crucified. Here's the History Behind This Brutal Practice," *Live Science*, April 19, 2019, https://www.livescience.com/65283-crucifixion-history.html.

3. Matteo Bevilacqua, Giulio Fanti, and Michele D'Arienzo, "The Causes of Jesus' Death in the Light of the Holy Bible and the Turin Shroud," *Open Journal of Trauma* 1, no. 2 (April 11, 2017): 37–46, https://doi.org/10.17352/ojt.000009.

4. Cahleen Shrier, PhD, "The Science of the Cross," Azusa Pacific University, accessed January 20, 2022, https://www.apu.edu/articles/the-science-of-the-crucifixion/.

LESSON 8

1. Some of this material was summarized from the article by Josh McDowell, "Evidence for the Resurrection," Josh McDowell: A Cru Ministry, accessed January 20, 2022, https://www.josh.org/wp-content/uploads/Evidence-For-The-Resurrection.pdf.

2. Randy Alcorn, "The Evidence for Christ's Resurrection," Eternal Perspectives Ministries, April 3, 2021, https://www.epm.org/blog/2021/Apr/3/evidence-christs-resurrection.

3. John Ankerberg and John Weldon, *Handbook of Biblical Evidences* (Eugene, OR: Harvest House Publishers, 2008), 101.

4. "Adrian Rogers," AZ Quotes, accessed January 20, 2022, https://www.azquotes.com/quote/896387.

LESSON 9

1. Blue Letter Bible, s.v. "*kēphas*," accessed Janaury 4, 2022, https://www.blueletterbible.org/lexicon/g2786/kjv/tr/0-1/.

LESSON 11

1. Lawrence R. Farley, *The Gospel of Matthew: The Torah for the Church* (Chesterton, IN: Conciliar Press, 2009).

2. "Latest Bible Translation Statistics," Wycliffe Bible Translators, accessed January 11, 2022, https://www.wycliffe.org.uk/about/our-impact/.

3. "Best-Selling Book," Guinness World Records, accessed January 20, 2022, https://www.guinnessworldrecords.com/world-records/best-selling-book-of-non-fiction.

LESSON 12

1. *Merriam-Webster*, s.v. "anno Domini," accessed January 4, 2022, https://www.merriam-webster.com/dictionary/anno%20Domini.

LESSON 14

1. Randy Alcorn, *Life Promises for Eternity* (Carol Stream, IL: Tyndale House, 2012), 193.

LESSON 15

1. Bible Study Tools, s.v. *"ekklesia,"* accessed January 20, 2022, https://www. biblestudytools.com/lexicons/greek/nas/ekklesia.html.
2. Blue Letter Bible, s.v. *"koinōnia,"* accessed January 4, 2022, https://www. blueletterbible.org/lexicon/g2842/kjv/tr/0-1/.

LESSON 16

1. Bible Study Tools, s.v. *"eucharistia,"* accessed January 20, 2022, https:// www.biblestudytools.com/lexicons/greek/nas/eucharistia.html.

LESSON 18

1. Bible Study Tools, s.v. *"koinonia,"* accessed January 20, 2022, https://www. biblestudytools.com/lexicons/greek/nas/koinonia.html.
2. "St. Augustine of Hippo," *Catholic Digest,* accessed September 28, 2020, https://www.catholicdigest.com/amp/from-the-magazine/quiet-moment/ st-augustine-of-hippo-to-fall-in-love-with-god/.

LESSON 19

1. John Wesley, QuoteFancy, accessed January 17, 2022, https://quotefancy. com/quote/1464625/John-Wesley-Sing-lustily-and-with-a-good-courage- Beware-of-singing-as-if-you-were-half.

LESSON 20

1. "130 Prince Quotes That Reign Over Creativity & Music," Quote Ambition, accessed January 20, 2022, https://www.quoteambition.com/prince-quotes/.
2. "Oscar Wilde Quotes," Goodreads, accessed January 20, 2022, https://www. goodreads.com/quotes/363232-the-only-way-to-get-rid-of-temptation-is-to.
3. "Mae West," BrainyQuote, accessed January 17, 2022, https://www. brainyquote.com/quotes/mae_west_130791.

LESSON 21

1. "Corrie ten Boom," AZ Quotes, accessed January 17, 2022, https://www. azquotes.com/quote/367527.
2. "Martin Luther Quotes," BrainyQuote, accessed January 17, 2022, https:// www.brainyquote.com/quotes/martin_luther_385793.

LESSON 23

1. "Nehemiah 1:1," NASB Study Bible (Grand Rapids, MI: Zondervan Publishing House, 1999), 655.
2. Bible Study Tools, s.v. *"paraclete,"* accessed January 20, 2022, https://www. biblestudytools.com/dictionary/paraclete/.

3. Bible Tools, s.v. *"anakainosis,"* accessed January 20, 2022, https://www.bibletools.org/index.cfm/fuseaction/Lexicon.show/ID/G342/anakainosis.htm.

4. "Dietrich Bonhoeffer Quotes," Goodreads, accessed January 18, 2022, https://www.goodreads.com/quotes/570188-fruit-is-always-the-miraculous-the-created-it-is-never.

5. *Merriam-Webster,* s.v. "consecration," accessed January 20, 2022, https://www.merriam-webster.com/dictionary/consecrate.

LESSON 24

1. "How Was the Bible Distributed Before the Printing Press Was Invented in 1455?," Biblica, accessed January 20, 2022, https://www.biblica.com/resources/bible-faqs/how-was-the-bible-distributed-before-the-printing-press-was-invented-in-1455/.

2. "Latest Bible Translation Statistics," Wycliffe Bible Translators, accessed January 18, 2022, https://www.wycliffe.org.uk/about/our-impact/.

3. Charles Spurgeon, *The Complete Works of C. H. Spurgeon,* vol. 35 (Harrington, DE: Delmarva Publications, 2015), sermon 2084.

LESSON 25

1. Merlin Carothers, *Prison to Praise* (Alachua, FL: Logos International, 1970).

LESSON 26

1. "Historical Estimates of World Population," US Census Bureau, accessed January 20, 2022, https://www.census.gov/data/tables/time-series/demo/international-programs/historical-est-worldpop.html.

2. Zach Dawes Jr., "Christian Percentage of Global Population to Increase," Good Faith Media, January 11, 2021, https://goodfaithmedia.org/christian-percentage-of-global-population-to-increase/.

3. "Charles Spurgeon," AZ Quotes, accessed January 20, 2022, https://www.azquotes.com/quote/544838.

4. Quoted in Samuel Ashton Keen, *Pentecostal Papers or, The Gift of the Holy Ghost* (Cincinnati: Cranston & Curts, 1895), 72.

LESSON 27

1. "Charles Spurgeon Quotes," AZ Quotes, accessed January 19, 2022, https://www.azquotes.com/quote/868178.

LESSON 29

1. The bulleted material was summarized or sourced from Tim Challies, "3 Awful Features of Roman Sexual Morality," *Challies* (blog), October 17,

2016, https://www.challies.com/articles/3-awful-features-of-roman-sexual-morality/.
2. Carmen Niethammer, "Cracking the $150 Billion Business of Human Trafficking," *Forbes*, February 2, 2020, https://www.forbes.com/sites/carmenniethammer/2020/02/02/cracking-the-150-billion-business-of-human-trafficking/?sh=7ddaea194142.

About the Author

J. LEE GRADY served for years as a Christian journalist before he became a full-time traveling minister. He worked at *Charisma* magazine from 1992–2010 and served as editor for eleven of those years. In 2000 he launched The Mordecai Project—an international humanitarian organization dedicated to helping women and girls who suffer from various forms of abuse and oppression. Today The Mordecai Project sponsors projects in Latin America, Africa, and Asia to bring the healing of Jesus Christ to those suffering from gender-based violence and discrimination. Grady's missionary work has taken him to thirty-six countries. Find out more at themordecaiproject.org.

Grady's previous books include *Follow Me, 10 Lies the Church Tells Women, The Truth Sets Women Free, 10 Lies Men Believe, Fearless Daughters of the Bible, The Holy Spirit Is Not for Sale*, and *Set My Heart on Fire*—a Bible study about the Holy Spirit. He also writes a weekly column, "Fire in My Bones," which is read by thousands of subscribers to *Charisma*. You can access it for free at fireinmybones.com.

Since 2010 Grady has had a special mandate to disciple and mentor young adults and emerging ministry leaders. He does this through regional Bold Venture retreats for both men and women as well as through individual mentoring. This book and *Follow Me* are direct outgrowths of his discipleship ministry. You can learn more about Grady at leegrady.com.

If you'd like more information about The Mordecai Project or any of Grady's ministries, email themordecaiproject@gmail.com or write to:

The Mordecai Project / Bold Venture Ministries
PO Box 2781
LaGrange, GA 30241

Read all these inspirational books by J. Lee Grady:

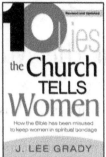

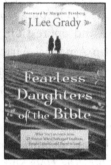

Dear reader,

Thank you for reading my book. I'm thrilled you decided to use *Let's Go Deeper* as your chosen discipleship tool. I hope it has strengthened your faith in Jesus and helped you effectively lead others in their relationship with Him.

Now that you've read *Let's Go Deeper*, be sure to read *Follow Me*, the original discipleship book that this practical guide came from. This book can be used by individuals or churches to gain a clear and simple discipleship strategy. Prepare to get outside your comfort zone and discover what God wants to do with you!

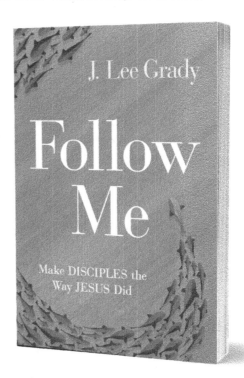

J. Lee Grady

Follow Me

Make DISCIPLES the Way JESUS Did

God bless,

Lee Grady

Whether you are studying *Let's Go Deeper* by yourself or with a small group, you can enhance your study with the *Let's Go Deeper* video series. Grady offers a five-minute video introduction to each lesson so you can gain additional biblical insights and hear his refreshing and relevant applications on each topic. Just go to **leegrady.com/godeeper**.